In Performance

EDITED BY
CAROL MARTIN

In Performance is a book series devoted to national and global theater of the twenty-first century. Scholarly essays providing the theatrical, cultural, and political contexts for the plays and performance texts introduce each volume. The texts are written both by established and emerging writers, translated by accomplished translators and aimed at people who want to put new works on stage, read diverse dramatic and performance literature and study diverse theater practices, contexts, and histories in light of globalization.

In Performance has been supported by translation and editing grants from the following organizations:

The Book Institute, Krakow
TEDA Project, Istanbul
The Memorial Fund for Jewish Culture, New York
Polish Cultural Institute, New York
Zbigniew Raszewski Theatrical Institute, Warsaw

SOLUM

AND OTHER PLAYS
FROM TURKEY

Edited by **Serap Erincin**

Translated by **Serap Erincin**
and **Mark Ventura**

LONDON NEW YORK CALCUTTA

This publication was supported by a grant from
the TEDA Translation Subvention Project, Ministry of Culture
and Tourism, Republic of Turkey.

Seagull Books 2011

ISBN-13 978 0 8574 2 001 5

British Library Cataloging-in-Publication Data
A catalog record for this book is available from the British Library

Designed by Bishan Samaddar, Seagull Books, Calcutta, India
Printed and bound by Hyam Enterprises, Calcutta, India

CONTENTS

For my first friend, Birgül Erincin,
and all the other children of the junta.

Serap Erincin

I am enormously grateful to the visionary Carol Martin, the architect of *In Performance* series who asked me to edit this volume, and to publisher Naveen Kishore whose kindness and warmth reaches over continents, for allowing these plays and the issues in Turkey voiced through their performances to reach a much wider audience. My thanks to all the authors for generously sharing their brilliant work. Infinite gratitude goes to Mark Ventura, who diligently translated these plays with me, and edited them with extreme attention to detail; without his mind and talent, these plays would not have come into being in English.

Thank you to all the directors, photographers, producers, performers, and institutions for supplying performance details and photographs. Thank you to Mariellen Sanford for editing the introduction. Thank you to everyone at Seagull Books. I am grateful to the Turkish Ministry of Culture, especially Müge Doğanay, for its contribution to this project with a TEDA grant.

The plays compiled in this volume are a few among many great plays. Thanks to all who offered their work and suggestions, especially Şule Ateş and Şafak Uysal. I owe a very special thanks to Dikmen Gürün, the mastermind of the Istanbul International Theater Festival, who supported countless plays, including several in this book, and to Cevza Sevgen for her efforts in preserving space for performance in and through the academia in Turkey.

Thank you, all my teachers past and present. My incredible advisors Richard Schechner, Deborah Kapchan, and André Lepecki have been a constant source of inspiration and support. I cannot imagine any word can grasp the magnitude of my gratitude. Diana Taylor, José Muñoz, and Michael Taussig have been major influences. It was a pleasure to study with Barbara Browning, Chris McGahan,

Karen Shimakawa, Tavia Nyong'o, Karen Finley, Dan Gerould, and Elizabeth LeCompte. Thanks to everyone at Performance Studies: it is a privilege to be in the company of so many wonderful people and minds as colleagues. Thank you, especially, Noel Rodriguez, for being the most amazing administrator. Thank you, all former colleagues, mentors, and students at Boğaziçi, Kumpanya, NTV, CNBC, BBC and various colleges in New York. Sultan Catto and Myrna Chase have offered genuine support in my first year in New York, I owe you endless gratitude. Thank you those in Pottsville who have treated me kindly.

My wonderful friends all around the world—their names too many to write here—but you know who you are and I am thankful from the bottom of my heart for your existence. Special thanks to Barış Celiloğlu and Emma Levine of London, and Pelin Uzay, Ece Aykol, and Stefanos Tsigrimanis of New York: your intellectual and warm presences were vital in critical moments at home away from home. My family, tighter than blood, Vedat, Pınar, Akasya, Deniz, Birgül, Mehtap, Burhan, Feriha Erincin, I love you so much. Selçuk Büyükbayrak, Elif Ayan, Ebru Ünal, Başak Kısakürek, Gülbin İrice, Zeynep Karagöz, Özge Kocabayoğlu, Berna Güroğlu, Dafne Kısakürek—you are my family; thank you for being my life support.

The last few years have been filled with a lot of sorrow as well as wonders. I am ever thankful for the magical and inspiring presence of Gizmo and Mark who share my every moment, for even on days filled with tears a glimpse of you will lighten my soul. You are my heart and my life.

Serap Erincin

The thirtieth anniversary of the most significant day in Turkey's recent history was marked in 2010. On September 12, 1980, Kenan Evren, then Chief of General Staff in the Turkish Army, led a coup d'état that brought an end to the civilian government and dissolved the parliament. Evren established a military dictatorship and was head of state until 1983.[1] The few bloody years following the coup and the oppressive events associated with that time are generally referred to collectively as "September 12th." During this time, hundreds of thousands of people were arrested; thousands were stripped of their citizenship, tortured, blacklisted, or made to disappear; tens of thousands fled the country as political refugees. That day and the years that followed haunt the memories and lives of millions and still reverberate in the policies and the constitution imposed on the country in 1982—a restrictive and authoritarian document, in sharp contrast to the 1961 constitution established to protect the rights of the citizens. The biggest problems facing Turkey today are either direct consequences of this period, or have been exacerbated by it. September 12th is a wound that will not begin to heal until its oppressive policies are reversed.

This volume presents six plays from Turkey, all of which premiered between 2003 and 2008. Although stylistically, aesthetically, and structurally diverse, they all address the current sociopolitical climate in Turkey and resonate with its most pressing issues: the repression of free speech, widespread poverty, tension between political factions, and the grievances of the Kurds and Armenians. In the plays these issues are contextualized in ways

[1] The 1980 coup was complicated in terms of the conspicuous and inconspicuous forces that supported it, the economic and political reasons behind it, and its strategy, policy, and method. There is abundant research that deals with these issues in great detail.

specific to Turkey. But they are also global concerns: human rights violations and the failure of a government to represent its people. To understand the factors that inspired these plays, what they mean to the people of Turkey, what they say to their spectators and their imagined audiences, and to situate them in the political, economic, cultural, and sociological context of the present moment, one needs to appreciate the scope of the trauma of September 12th.

Immediately after the establishment of the modern Turkish Republic in 1923, there were failed attempts to institute a multi-party system that would create an opposition to the ruling Republican People's Party (Cumhuriyet Halk Fırkası [CHF], later Cumhuriyet Halk Partisi [CHP]) established by the founder of Turkey, Mustafa Kemal Atatürk. Finally, following the Second World War, the Democrat Party (Demokrat Parti [DP]) was formed. In 1950, the CHP lost the parliamentary election to the DP, winning only 69 seats to the DP's 408—a clear mandate for change. The DP supported private entrepreneurship and foreign capital. It also allowed religion to have a wider presence in public institutions and implemented other policies affecting public life that were markedly different from those of the CHP. For instance, after 1932, following a series of reforms favoring Westernization and secularization, the *azan* (the Islamic call for prayer) had to be in Turkish. Considering that the majority of the people in Turkey do not speak or understand Arabic, this seemingly made sense. But while this was part of a broad effort to reinforce the use of a "pure" Turkish vocabulary (like other influential nationalist policies of this period all over Europe that were geared toward building nation-states), it was insensitive to the Muslim people's spiritual attachment to these words as divine concepts. In 1950, the DP ruled to allow the *azan* to be recited in Arabic, and thus won the hearts and votes of religious conservatives.

However, it was not much later that the DP itself began a campaign of oppression. It silenced opposing politicians; the press was censored and prosecuted if they were critical of the government. These changes kindled public support for the first of several military interventions—in other words, coups—that undermined democracy in Turkey. The 1960 revolution of May 27, led by young officers, successfully broke the chain of command. But it had some violent consequences, including the execution of then prime minister and DP leader, Adnan Menderes. Ironically, it also led to the 1961 constitution, which focused on human rights and freedom of expression. This constitution established the separation of powers, independent judicial bodies, and freedom of expression for individuals and groups. While there were changes made to this democratic constitution during the 1970s, it was in effect until the coup in 1980. Every problem that contemporary Turkey has to deal with has been complicated by the 1982 constitution which came out of this coup. One of these is the unresolved Kurdish issue—the contested rights of the significant Kurdish minority in Turkey.[2] It has been notably difficult for the Kurdish population to secure political representation.[3]

---

2 The roots of the conflict go back to the Ottoman times. The violent conflict between the Turkish military and the Kurdistan Workers Party (PKK), which is recognized as a terrorist group by the US and Europe, has cost over 40,000 lives since the 1980s.

As a continuation of the early twentieth-century nation-state movement in Europe, Turkey adopted (some even before the foundation of modern Turkey) several radical measures, such as changing all non-Turkish names of places to Turkish ones. Such nationalist actions denied the Kurdish their independent identity. The military rule of the 1980s extended the oppression to the point of denying recognition of the Kurds as a separate ethnicity. Kurds in Turkey were even forbidden to give their children Kurdish names or play Kurdish music.

3 A party must receive a minimum of 10 percent of the total national vote for its candidates to occupy seats in the parliament even if a candidate wins a majority in her or his district. In the 2006 elections, Kurdish politicians were able to establish a small presence in the parliament by circumventing the election law: they ran as independent candidates, and were therefore not subject to the 10-percent rule. They formed a "group" (a minimum of 20 members is required to form a group) in the parliament allowing them representation in the executive councils and other commissions. However, the group faced threats of dissolution several times and was eventually dissolved in December 2009.

The debate between the radically secular and the religious is yet another conflict, and it was heightened with the ban on wearing the headscarf. Women in Turkey cannot attend college or work in government buildings while wearing an Islamic headscarf. The law regards this not as individual freedom but as a breach of secularity. As a result, some women have not been able to attend college. The tension between the staunchly secular and the religious conservatives of the ruling Adalet ve Kalkınma Partisi (AKP)[4] sharply escalated after the government tried to lift the ban on wearing headscarves in universities in Turkey, and before that, in 2007, when they nominated (and eventually elected) the current president of Turkey, Abdullah Gül. The protests against Gül's nomination were rooted partly in the fact that AKP imposed his presidency—he was not the preferred candidate for many because of his Islamist background and past statements that were deemed less than favorable toward a secular regime.

This fear of a Sharia regime is one of the reasons the military has been able to retain its power in Turkey. The military in Turkey has been staunchly secular. It is also very powerful, partially because it was primarily the military leaders who, after a long war, rebuilt the country in 1923 out of the dissolved Ottoman Empire. In the eyes of many, especially those who witnessed the conse-quences of the Iranian revolution of 1979, the military is the main protection against the threat of a Sharia regime in Turkey. Some see this as insurance for the survival of secularism; others see it as a major roadblock for the personal and political freedoms normally associated with a democracy: freedom of religion, freedom of speech, the right to protest, and even the right to speak your native language. The oppressive mentality of the junta regime has

---

4 The main opposing party, CHP, identifies itself as highly secular, and the AKP, the party of the current Prime Minister Recep Tayyip Erdoğan, is regarded as religiously conservative, although it denies that it has such an agenda. It does have several members who are not openly observant.

so deeply penetrated public consciousness that anti-democratic practices such as oppression and censorship have become the norm in the minds of Turkey's people. State institutions established after September 12th control previously independent organs like education and the media. As a result, the people of Turkey have become less reactive, less political, and, most importantly, less tolerant.

Identity crisis, chaos, and confusion define the current state of affairs in Turkey. There is too much contradiction. It is confusing to defend lifting the ban on headscarves when one is against oppression of women in different forms (that is, if you view obligatory headscarves in Muslim society as a form of oppression). It is confusing to see a prime minister who claims to argue for free speech sue journalists who are critical of him; to see people who claim to support leftist principles (like championing the rights of the proletariat) defend military involvement in the administration of the country; to see those who actively support gender equality or work for better treatment of gays and lesbians vehemently resist expansion of representation rights for ethnic minorities in Turkey.

All of the performance texts in this volume share in an effort to address questions of identity, but they vary greatly in style, in their use of language, and their production values. As such, they demonstrate a broad spectrum of aesthetics. The plays collected in this volume have generated some of the most recognized productions created by artists from Turkey in recent years. I am not arguing that these are the best, the most successful, or the six most popular plays from Turkey. Nor am I suggesting that these plays resulted in the best productions in Turkey. These plays represent only a small segment of the theater in Turkey. Still, each play is significant for its content and for the dramatic means of articulating its content. They have all been nationally and internationally performed and praised.

All but one of the plays in this anthology blend traditional and experimental techniques to different degrees. After the founding of the modern Turkish Republic in 1923, Westernization—used synonymously with "modernization"—was a primary objective in Turkey, in the arts as well as in many other areas of life. Roman letters replaced the Arabic alphabet and Western-style clothing was popularized. In theater practice, interpretations of the methods of Konstantin Stanislavsky were followed for many decades. Some traditional styles from the Ottoman Empire era were still performed— such as *orta oyunu*, which is similar to commedia dell'arte—but the state and city theaters for the most part tried to keep up with Western theater practices rather than create their own theater for their newly established country. Thus theater became almost exclusively associated with the West. The three military coups between 1960 and 1980 did not help the cultivation of arts. Artists, especially those who were deemed experimental or marginal, were among the worst affected during these oppressive times.

Until the 1980s it was difficult to argue for a distinct, authentic theater of Turkey. The classic conservatory education followed the Western tradition, and most theater practitioners and writers sought to stylistically copy the West. While the efforts toward founding a Western-style theater have helped establish a very powerful, well-funded, and institutionalized presence of live performance in Turkey, it has also limited the growth of original work. Beginning in the mid-1970s, new developments and experimentation in the art world started to have some influence in Turkey. The works of Peter Brook and Jerzy Grotowski were translated and reached a considerable audience. Several experimental companies emerged. It is, however, only in the last 10 to 15 years that one can clearly see an effort to develop a home-grown language of live performance in Turkey. There has been, in particular, a major boom in dance and dance theater in the last decade. Dancers, dance-theater performers, and choreographers from Turkey have taken their work to international venues, gaining wider recognition. Contemporary dance flourished more freely than theater in Turkey as it was not, like theater, burdened with having to overcome an imposing Western aesthetic. Theater practitioners still had to find their own freedom and form.

Istanbul is the host of one of the major theater festivals in Europe. The festival took place every year between 1989 and 2002 and since then has been held only biennially owing to financial limitations. The festival is directed by Dikmen Gürün, one of the most influential theater personalities in Turkey. Thanks to this festival, artists and students in Turkey have had the chance to be exposed to performances exhibiting a wide spectrum of styles, techniques, and aesthetics, contributing significantly to breaking down the rigorous formality of conservative styles in theater in Turkey.

Artists, like the rest of the people in Turkey, have long been conflicted over the dichotomy between the West and the East, or rather between Europe and the Middle East. Turkish citizens have only recently begun to find unique ways to express theatrical and aesthetic identity. Turkey is, on so many levels, at a crossroad: of cultures, climates, traditions, continents, the East and the West. Even the seven regions that comprise Turkey are distinct from one another. Their geography, climate, cuisine, dialect, cultural, and social traditions are vastly different. For many years, only Western aesthetics were represented in art; if Middle Eastern or Mediterranean influences made an appearance, it was usually to show how backward these influences were.

Of the six texts represented in this volume, three—*Home Sweet Home*, *As on the Page*, and *Solum*—focus on constructing the visual image on the stage. The other three plays are more language-based and more conventionally structured: *Eurydice's Cry* was adapted from Sophocles's *Antigone*, while *For Rent* and *Avalanche* are original texts. *Home Sweet Home*, *As on the Page*, and *Solum* mesh contemporary techniques with elements of more traditional performance from Turkey, such as storytelling. *Eurydice's Cry*,

xvi

SERAP ERİNCİN

Home Sweet Home, *Solum*, and *As on the Page* involve stylized or choreographed movement or dance. *Home Sweet Home* and *As on the Page* utilize documentary performance techniques, such as sound clips from interviews or narrating facts (e.g., Eastern traditions). *Home Sweet Home* is an interactive multimedia work.

The artists who have created these works were born in three different eras. Tuncer Cücenoğlu (*Avalanche*) was born in 1944; Murathan Mungan (*As on the Page*) in 1955; Şahika Tekand (*Eurydice's Cry*) in 1959; Mustafa Kaplan (*Solum*) and Özen Yula (*For Rent*) in 1965; and Emre Koyuncuoğlu (*Home Sweet Home*) in 1966. The authors come from different backgrounds, both socially and artistically. Even though they all spend most of their time in Istanbul now, they grew up in different parts of Turkey. All of them—except Yula, who attended high school in the US as part of an exchange program—graduated from secondary schools in the cities where they were born. While this was not at all a deciding factor in selecting the plays for this volume, it contributes to their intrinsic diversity, which *was* important in their selection. Mungan is from Mardin, the very south-east of Turkey; Yula is from Gaziantep, also in the south-east but a larger city close to the middle Anatolian/Mediterranean region; Tekand is from İzmir, another metropolitan city in the Aegean region or Western Turkey; Kaplan is from Konya, the heartland; and Cücenoğlu is from Çorum, another inland city, closer to the north. The only artist here who was born and who grew up in Istanbul is Koyuncuoğlu.

The geographic and generational diversity of the six playwrights is reflected in the wide range of issues in these pages: questions involving secularity, the headscarf, junta regimes, free speech, the independence of the judiciary, access to the European Union, human rights, queer rights, women's rights, violence against women, minority rights, gender inequality, torture, the disappeared, displacement, immigration, economic inequities, and class. To generalize, all the works grapple with questions of identity and the fight for freedom of expression, each one contributing to restoring to Turkey tolerance of 'the other'—a virtue that has gradually diminished throughout the country.

In this volume, no one play explicitly or solely speaks about gender inequality, women's rights, or queer rights, yet these concerns are present. One of the plays, *For Rent*, written by one of the most popular playwrights in Turkey, has never been performed in the country, arguably because it depicts sexual relations between men and uses explicit dialogue without being *about* queer relationships. Not only are there no anti-discriminatory laws to protect queer citizens but they are also not afforded the same rights and protection as other citizens. While there have been improvements in the penal code, the code is still far from protecting all its citizens equally.

Theater in Turkey has started directing more attention to social issues lately, especially regarding honor crimes. Men receive lighter sentences for crimes against women, particularly when they claim "honor" as the pretext for the crime. In the past, honor crimes, violation of women's rights, and any infringements of queer rights were afforded less visibility because it was thought that they took place only in certain sections of the population. Whereas, in fact, the perpetrators of these offenses hailed from everywhere: they were Kurds, Turks, Armenians, rich and poor, uneducated and intellectual, nationalist and socialist. My hope is that in theater and in other intellectual practices, in both the art world and in academia, the issues of all marginalized people in this mostly conservative society will be brought forward as problems for the entire nation to rectify, just as the plays in this volume bring to light the oppression of and the infringement on the rights of all minorities.

As on the Page by Murathan Mungan is a play from the trilogy *Paper Rock Cloth*, first published in Turkey in 2007.[5]

---

5 *As on the Page* refers to the "Paper" segment of the trilogy.

Mungan's use of the Turkish language is very sophisticated, and in translation it is difficult to do justice to the poetry of his text and preserve the veiled revolt against the authoritarian nationalist establishment subtly evident in his choice of vocabulary, which recognizes Turkey's diverse past and present.[6] In production, *As on the Page* incorporates methods of storytelling that are an important part of the performance traditions of Anatolia (Asia Minor), such as Meddah and shadow play. The play reveals subtle cultural details of Eastern Anatolia that are perhaps unknown even to most who are from that region. While Mungan was writing this play, he visualized every aspect of how it would be performed, like an auteur writer/director (even though he does not direct his plays). Through a character named "Text Narrator" he describes in detail how the performance should be staged. The characeter named "Narrator" walks the readers through the lighting and blocking of the performance as he tells the story of the play. His words describe the actions on the stage and interpret their meaning and significance. Through this device Mungan prescribes every action and situation to accompany his lines; however, he also leaves it up to the director whether or not to include this character in the performance. So, despite these particular details integrated into the text, the play still offers the potential director and performers complete freedom.

Avalanche has the most conventional dramatic structure of the plays in this anthology: it is a play in three acts, with unity of time, place, and action, with stereotypical characters. Cücenoğlu calls his characters Man, Woman, Young Man, etc. His focus is on presenting an action that is symbolic of an oppressive society,

---

6 Mungan abundantly uses words that were replaced in efforts to "purify" the Turkish language from other influences (the Ottoman language, often referred to as Old Turkish, was a mixture of Turkish, Arabic, and Persian). This gesture brings rich sounds to his work, but it is also a political stance. By claiming this vocabulary, used in Turkey for hundreds of years, Mungan proclaims ownership of the diversity that is inherent not only in the language but also in the culture.

specifically *his* society during *his* lifetime. The play presents an ideal to those living under oppression: people should take action regarding their future instead of living in fear. Cücenoğlu's play is part of the pressure on the government to take action regarding the growing human rights violations in Turkey. Interestingly, the play has been produced a lot among countries that were formerly parts of the erstwhile USSR, including Russia.

The play is set in a mountain village that lives under the threat of an avalanche for nine months of the year. During those nine months, people take extreme measures to prevent an avalanche; for example, they bury women alive who may give birth before the threat of the avalanche is over as the cries of a newborn baby and a woman in labor may trigger one. Fear and suppression permeate villagers' lives to the point that, even in the months when there is no threat, they cannot go back to normal. The threat of the avalanche functions like a junta regime's administration in the creation of a culture of fear. Even today, Turkish citizens do not trust the police but, rather, live in fear of being "disappeared" or prosecuted for expressing their political beliefs. The best way to stay out of trouble is to bury and disappear the voices of disturbance. *Avalanche* suggests that, while staying quiet may help one to stay out of immediate danger, it does little to address abiding problems. Sooner or later, everyone will be affected by the threats that cause their fear, as they are stripped of their humanity and lose the ability to live a normal life.

While *Avalanche* addresses the effects of communal oppression, *Eurydice's Cry* looks at individual oppression. There are references throughout the play to military rule and martial law under the junta regime of Kenan Evren (the leader of September 12th, now past 90 but still vilified by many) and represented in the play by Creon. Tekand rewrote her version of *Antigone* to voice concerns about the right of the other, freedom of expression, religious freedom, the just practice of the law, ethnic battles, and war[7]—all considerations weighing heavily on the people of Turkey at present.

In the play there is a direct parallel between Antigone's desire to bury her brother and the desire of women in Turkey to be able to cover their heads while attending college. Both are trying to perform what they see as a sacred duty and a human right. In both cases, women are faced with a dilemma: they have to choose to obey either the rules of their religion or the law. Antigone calls this a "sacred crime:" "I won't obey a law that takes away my most natural right."[8] For this Antigone, "Laws are to protect rights, not to seize them!"

Tekand is implicitly identifying and protesting Turkish law: it is based not on human rights, but on the *limitation* of human rights as stipulated in the UN's Universal Declaration of Human Rights. *Eurydice's Cry* portrays the law that abridges an individual's right to perform her faith as a violation of a basic human right. Antigone's future husband, Haemon, is very clear about what should be done to the 1982 constitution and its articles violating human rights: "If a law has become the tool of atrocity instead of justice it should be thrown away like a rotten organ!" Haemon speaks for many individuals in Turkey who fear being prosecuted for expressing their beliefs: "The whole city can see the truth. But they are scared to raise their voices!" The possible consequences of Article 301—which makes it illegal to speak out against anything Turkish, including the government—looms over *Eurydice's Cry* like the avalanche in Cücenoğlu's play. *Eurydice's Cry* is the scream of those who are afraid to raise their voices yet can no longer remain silent. *Eurydice's Cry* ends on a very grim note, quite different from the hopeful ending of *Avalanche*. However, the plays share a similar activist message. In *Avalanche*, this is reinforced through the

---

7 Program notes from *Eurydice's Cry*, June 2006.

8 All quotes, unless otherwise indicated, are my translations.

action; in *Eurydice's Cry*, it is proclaimed by Eurydice who breaks her silence in agony upon losing her son: "Damn the happiness caused by obedience!"

Eurydice's Cry preserves the classical structure of ancient Greek plays and the text dictates very little about the production. Tekand's own production used lighting, choreography, and sound to tell the story, so that the action of the play could be followed even if one could not speak Turkish and the issues would translate to delimitation of rights that affect people everywhere.

Özen Yula explained that news stories about an escalation in scams and robberies throughout the city—crimes brought on by the pressures of current economic conditions—inspired him to write *For Rent*.[9] He took as his starting point a story about the economically disenfranchised urban immigrants who promised sex but then robbed their clients. According to official numbers as of 2008, Turkey has a population of 71,517,100.[10] Of these, 75 per cent live in the cities and town centers. This is in stark contrast to the distribution of the population before 1980. Some of this is due to the global increase in population but the main reason is the search for economic opportunities that can create a better life. Most of these immigrants end up living in poverty, either in some of the neighborhoods far from the center or in new settlements built on the outskirts of the city.[11] So, while the numbers suggest that 75 percent of the population lives in cities, a large part of that population lives in substandard dwellings removed from the urban infrastructure in geographic locations that are vulnerable to natural disasters such as floods. Disparity in the distribution of wealth and

---

9 Personal correspondence with Özen Yula, October 2008.

10 These numbers are taken from the reports of Turkish Statistical Institute, Prime Ministry of Turkey (http://www.tuik.gov.tr).

11 A considerable percentage of this population live in the slums in illegal housing they built themselves, called the *gecekondu*, meaning "placed at night"—implying the quick construction of these houses without permission or permits.

economic power creates tension that, as one might expect, lead to crime. *For Rent* portrays the possible consequences of such difficult economic conditions. What is most striking about *For Rent* is that it is able to present stark realities through high theatricality. For instance, certain characters have surreal monologues which they speak after their death or from a distant future. The entire performance takes place in a city park that is like a microcosm of the world and where most of the characters meet one another for the first time. The characters are outcasts who have nothing to lose, who risk their bodies and their lives for very little in return. Their language is brutal and shocking and their action is violent as they cut one another with razor blades. Yula said[12] that he wanted to portray everything from the vantage point of those on the periphery—the "others." He asks some basic, philosophical questions: Why would one person rob or harm another? What are the reasons? What forces someone to do this? He constructed the play in cinematic fashion with these questions in mind. For instance, he created the character of the 14-year-old prostitute and then he aged the character; next, he wrote the character of the gigolo she falls in love with, and added his murder; and then character of the the old man who killed him was developed.

According to Yula, urban inhabitants throughout the world can identify with the problems of the play's characters. As cities grow, so do their problems; and when the economy deteriorates, everything starts to crumble. What we call "civilization" today thrives only when and if all the people of a city are allowed to live in humane conditions. For Yula, "Indeed, this is the concern of the play. We are tired of watching the love and familial problems of the middle class. Let's take a look at the situation of those people they do not care about."[13] In Istanbul, as in many parts of the world, the impoverished people are the majority.

---

12 Personal correspondence with Özen Yula, October 2008.
13 Ibid.

Home Sweet Home, a site-specific documentary performance, brings up a few of the most contested issues in Turkey, ranging from the atrocities involving the Armenian Ottomans during the First World War[14] to the continuing Kurdish conflict. *Home Sweet Home* was first performed in an abandoned Armenian church in the predominantly Kurdish south-eastern city of Diyarbakır, an extremely impoverished region. In every city where it was performed, *Home Sweet Home* was recreated in a location that was significant to the past and present of that city. Koyuncuoğlu prefers places that were once a vital part of daily life but have now been abandoned, places that were used by different cultures but then changed or lost their identities. The play interrogates the concepts of home, house, and land, all of which are extremely important in a geography where Armenians, Kurds, and Turks (among others) have been continually displaced.[15] However, given the scope of conflicts throughout the world and countless populations displaced because of violence, poverty, or political unrest, *Home Sweet Home* reverberates with themes that are globally relevant.

---

14 This refers to events during the First World War, widely referred to as the "Armenian Genocide." While Turkey insists that the deaths in 1915 were the results of atrocities of war, it also makes the argument that these things happened before the foundation of Turkey in 1923. After generations of hostilities, in October 2009, a peace treaty was signed between Armenia and Turkey. This was the first step in restoring diplomacy and opening the border between the two countries. Turkey had closed its border with Armenia in 1993 during the conflict between Azerbaijan and Armenia.

15 Many ethnic groups lived together in Asia Minor and south-eastern Europe during the Ottoman Empire. After the First World War, which also encompasses Turkey's war for independence, in accordance with the Lausanne Treaty (1923), the Christian (Greek) citizens in Turkey (excluding those in Istanbul and the islands of Gökçeada and Bozcaada), and the Muslim (Turkish) citizens in Greece (excluding those in Western Thrace)—totaling two million people—were forced to emigrate: the Greeks to Greece, the Turks to Turkey. These are not issues of a distant past: a look at the statistics of the Istanbul riots of 1955 confirms their relevance. Upon receiving news that the Turkish consulate in Thessaloniki, Greece (incidentally the birthplace of Atatürk), had been bombed, Istanbul's Greek community—those who were allowed to remain after the exchange—were assaulted. Only 10 people died, but the fear of hatred this provoked was immeasurable. At that time there were almost 150,000 Greeks in Turkey; by 1978 this number had dwindled to 7,000.

Home Sweet Home is inspired by real events and real places. The text comprises dialogue recorded during interviews with people of different ages, sexes, and regions. In her program note from 2003, Koyuncuoğlu writes that the edited and reassembled words from these interviews were used as part of the performance text as anonymous oral history. She mentions that everyone spoke in their interviews of their homes and their homelands. There was a common recurrence in the interviews: when interviewees repeated a story, when they returned to something already discussed, frequently the story or the description changed according to the sentiment, situation, space, or the time elapsed; there was very little that was permanent in these oral accounts of history. Such observations alone are meditations on the concept of history, especially in a country where people are often deprived of formal education and hence there is little opportunity to learn about recent history, and where there is little tolerance for the narratives and accounts of others.

The aesthetic diversity of *Home Sweet Home* adds layers to the theme around the coexistence of different peoples. It blends contemporary dance and structured (traditional) folk dance, and video and interaction between performers and the community. Koyuncuoğlu strives through her work to propose a new theater— one that speaks about today and embraces all the people of Turkey; one that creates its own space, its own design, its own concept of staging, and its own spectator; and, perhaps most importantly, one that is explicitly for the people of Turkey.

Aesthetically and conceptually there are examples of site-specific multimedia interactive documentary performances elsewhere in the world that pre-date *Home Sweet Home*. However, Koyuncuoğlu's work is an example for other artists who want to make the theater their own, make it say things about *them*, *their* present moment, *their* here and now; creating their own spaces and designs, and spectators, they can make it belong to their own country.

For Rent, *Home Sweet Home*, and finally Mustafa Kaplan's *Solum*, are all conceptualized around the idea of home, or the lack or loss of it. In Latin, *solum* means solitary or single, ground or base, and country or land. While the broader sociological implications of "home" as a concept are dealt with explicitly in the former two productions, *Solum*, a solo show performed by Kaplan, is more subtle. In all three plays, questions rooted in the concept of home generate questions about identity, even though they propose to answer the questions through different techniques. *Solum* is partially autobiographical but structured in such a way that every performance can be recreated using elements from a different performer's or fictional character's biography. *Solum* is a map for that process and spectators witness the performer's search for traces of transformation and identity. It is a play that directly speaks to those who feel like they are "in between"—in between places and cultures, like Kaplan, and like a considerable part of the population of Turkey.

Solum asks questions of home through the physical research on the performer's body that tests the limits of stretching, enduring, and absorbing pain. For instance, in the beginning, Kaplan puts numerous rubber bands around his face—tight, they cut into his skin. In the script, he details the installation of each band, carefully mapping the features and explaining the action of the performer. During this process of reconfiguring, disfiguring, and reassembling his body, Kaplan creates a series of different bodies onstage by tracing and naming the transformation of the figure/character/body/person/thing. When the performer is no longer *like* anything, he names the character after their actions.[16] During the performance characters are revealed one by one to the spectators,

---

16 However, during the performance, the spectators do not have the script and do not know that Kaplan fabricated separate characters with different names, all represented by this body. They have a different cognitive process, one that is born through the act of spectatorship. Kaplan records the names of these characters as a trace line for practitioners who will recreate the performance using the text.

as the performer transforms from one to the other. This transformation from one thing to the other, this state of being like something and being exactly like nothing, mirrors the self-perception of a large part of the population of Turkey. Kaplan assembles all these characters/bodies into one persona.[17] The larger part of the urban population has migrated from rural areas or small towns; they have changed, lost, rebuilt, and then perhaps reconnected, with their homes or hometowns. At one point in *Solum*, Kaplan does a headstand in one corner of the performance space while singing a rural folk song. The folk songs that he sings when he finds home again in his body arise from the past he has carried with himself.

Kaplan says he started creating this play by asking if his body could be a place of belonging:

> When I was a kid, I used to find small, shiny stones and swallow them. I don't remember when I stopped doing this. A friend of mine tried to circumcise himself with a pair of pliers. I also remember that I tried to lick the lime off newly painted walls [. . . As] a group, we would stuff our noses with grass, and try to make them bleed. I don't know why we played all these games on the body. I guess it was more about playing, discovering and being curious than about making it hurt.[18]

For Kaplan, the body is a country governed by personal history and social conditions leading him to ask: Where do we belong? Where is home?

Turkey is a society of people who are still forced to identify with either the East or the West, the Middle East or Europe, as it physically stands between Africa, Europe, and the Middle East. It is, in fact, uniquely European *and* Mediterranean *and* Middle

---

17 Looking at Kaplan's background, it is easy to trace his identity in this assemblage. He grew up in Konya, in the heartland of Turkey, and then spent his entire professional life in Istanbul, the cultural capital of the country. He has also traveled widely with these performances.

18 Personal correspondence with Mustafa Kaplan, November 2007.

Eastern. A lot of Turkish citizens are descendants of those who migrated from inner Asia, the Balkans, and other lands. It neighbors a number of different countries with widely varied cultures, languages, and religions. It harbors all of these cultures: it is all of them, and none of them. It is like many of them, but not exactly any of them. It is also surrounded by never-ending conflict in the Middle East, the Balkans, and former Soviet territories. It is composed of, and brings together, people of different cultures. Turkey is unique; it does not need to identify as either here or there but right where it is. It is full of the diversity that comes with accommodating countless cultures for thousands of years. Turkey is the central column of the world, the East and the West, the North and the South. The plays in this volume represent the variety of work that comprises Turkey's theater today. These plays ask questions troubling this diverse country, and offer impressions of some of the many faces and places that make up the landscape of contemporary Turkey.

AS ON THE PAGE

MURATHAN MUNGAN

IMAGE 1.1 **At the end of the play, the words of the narrator are depicted. As they die, the characters' "heads fall onto each other's knees. They die as if falling asleep."**

(From the left) Kristian Halken, Charlotte Rathnov, Louise Herbert, Mads Riisom (in the background).

As on the Page, directed by Alan Lyddiard, Betty Nansen Theater, Copenhangen, 2003.

Photograph: hansen-hansen.com (*Courtesy*: *Betty Nansen Theater*).

CHARACTERS

NARRATOR

TEXT NARRATOR

MAN

WOMAN

FIRST WOMAN

SECOND WOMAN

NOTES ON THE PLAY

As on the Page premiered at the Betty Nansen Theater, Copenhagen, in February 2003, as part of the production of "1001 Nights NOW," with the following cast and crew:

Cast	Kristian Halken, Charlotte Rathnov, Louise Herbert, Mads Riisom
Director	Alan Lyddiard
Set Designer	Neil Murray
Light Designer	Tina MacHugh

NOTE TO THE DIRECTOR

It is up to you to decide whether or not Text Narrator will take part in the performance. The way the text is written, she translates almost every motion in the performance into word, describes to us the text, tells us what we have seen or what we will see.

Even if the play is otherwise performed exactly as it is written, the director may abridge the words of Text Narrator if so desired. Obviously, the playwright talks to the director through the character of Text Narrator. Almost every stage exit and scene change is communicated through her/him. This may make the performance a bit too heavy with text.

However, what is important is that, even if they are performed in a different style, the words of Text Narrator should be preserved in this form so that varied extensions, times, and even contradictions, can be achieved.

TRANSLATOR'S NOTE

Turkish pronouns are gender-neutral. We have designated the Text Narrator as female and the Narrator male.

AS ON THE PAGE
Murathan Mungan

TEXT NARRATOR. The performance space is empty. When the lights come up and illuminate the performance space, the spectator first meets a three-dimensional emptiness.

The spectators watch the emptiness for a while with the knowledge that they will be seeing something, that something will be said to them there. The spectators and the performance space regard one another. Love at first sight is experienced with the emptiness. When we are born and when we look.

(*Silence.*)

Then Narrator enters the performance space and takes his first steps in the emptiness. Thus, the footfalls of a story are heard . . . Then a wispy cloud of steam . . .

NARRATOR. These wispy clouds of steam come from the cauldrons where paper pulp is boiled. The paper that is needed for the story to be written. Those who tend the cauldrons and stir them very slowly add the passing time into the texture of the paper. The time in which they dwell, boiling the paper.

You can't see the cauldrons I am narrating. In the East, a story is not shown, it is told. Soon, you will see the paper too. Just as you see the steam. I can't say if you will be able to see what is written on it. Some pages are like emptiness. Giving meaning to a page is like giving meaning to emptiness . . .

What is written on it is made meaningful not only with words but also with time . . .

TEXT NARRATOR. A sheet of paper glides into the performance space, having sprouted wings. Folded down the middle, this sheet of paper becomes two leaves, four pages. Off this paper steams the hot vapor of the cauldrons it has been boiled in . . . It opens and closes its wings, then obscures a part of the performance space like a curtain. It is off-white. It has a tint of beige. Its texture is not smooth. Occasionally, it trembles. It is waiting for the time of the one who writes and that which is written.

(*Silence.*)

The silhouette of Narrator appears on the page.

NARRATOR. In the East, performance is born out of shadow. It finds its words. It erects its story. It shows what it can do. It multiplies the forks at the divergences in the path of destiny. It points at time and the unknown, then makes its mark, and departs.

TEXT NARRATOR. As the paper becomes two leaves, closing toward the middle, Narrator, whose silhouette we just saw, is revealed. Narrator steps forward and joins the performance.

NARRATOR. In the *Tales from One Thousand and One Nights*, women signal to the youths passing through the street. Only the women know the meanings of their signs. The signs of a secret language among women. Young men learn these signs by heart without knowing the meanings, and then go to another street, another house, and repeat them to another woman, who watches through a window. Women who have been confined to their houses communicate with one another in this way. Through these signs relayed by men.

TEXT NARRATOR. The silhouette of a woman appears on the page. She demonstrates her signs. As she narrates, glittering gold leaves, silver inlays, and marbled embellishments appear on the top and on the sides of the page. The page becomes colorful, lively. It is vivified. Narrator plays the part of a passing young man who imprints the signs in his memory through repetition.

Then he goes, repeats the signs he has learned to another woman whose silhouette has appeared on the other page. This time too, the same gold leaves, silver inlays, and marbled embellishments appear on the other page. Narrator pauses, becomes confused, tries to remember the sign, falters. He tries, erases his movement, tries again. As he falters, so do the the tinsel, the inlays, the engravings. The marbled embellishments no longer flow.

(*Silence.*)

Then the paper closes like a book. It becomes a vertical line that divides the stage down the middle. Two women are revealed, standing side by side, no longer silhouettes. They look into the emptiness, that is, us.

Silence.

NARRATOR. Some signs are lost along the way. As one goes, passes, sometimes the signs themselves get lost, sometimes their meanings . . . The signs change as they travel. Their destinations and origins, even the road traveled, are not the same.

FIRST WOMAN. The shadow does not stand still as it is on the page.

SECOND WOMAN. The writing does not stand still as it is on the page.

FIRST WOMAN. The page is two-dimensional. The emptiness, on the other hand, is three-dimensional.

SECOND WOMAN. Every page stands still in the emptiness.

FIRST WOMAN. The stage is an emptiness.

SECOND WOMAN. It is filled as it is on the page.

TEXT NARRATOR. The paper opens itself again. Two people proceed, one from the East, one from the West. They start reading the page, one from each side. The light cast onto the page by the light-bearers, who are standing to the rear of the performance space, causes their own silhouettes to fall onto the page. Sometimes the light-bearers bring the light closer to the page, sometimes they take it farther away. Mysterious, complicated characters fill the pages. As the signs and writing multiply, their passion increases. These two figures try to see one another. The paper starts moving left and right, up and down, not allowing this. It guards its back and front. They switch places. One becomes the East, the other the West. The only thing that switches places are the figures. The East and the West of the page stay the same.

As they try to read while dancing in front of and behind the page, they simultaneously vocalize.

> The page that carries
> is also the one that does not have a passage through
>
> left, in front of, and behind the page
> are the one that carries and the one that is carried
> switching places does not solve
> the problem between them.

TEXT NARRATOR. As the dance of the East and the West, light and shadow, continues, bells are heard, as though from a distance. This is the sound of caravan bells. The world is connected to itself by routes.

NARRATOR. In the old days, in the caravans that traveled long routes day and night, stories were told to pass the time. However, in stories, time does not pass. The caravans carry the tale from the East to the West.

FIRST WOMAN. Can a tale be carried?

SECOND WOMAN. As it is carried, what does it lose, what does it gain?

FIRST WOMAN. Is there a tale that can carry time?

SECOND WOMAN. Because the time in the East and the time in the West are not the same.

TEXT NARRATOR. The light-bearers illuminate a passing caravan. The caravan passes through the page. Over it or through it. If you shut your eyes against your dreams.

FIRST WOMAN. When the *Tales from One Thousand and One Nights* began, it was night, and the next day never came.

SECOND WOMAN. What does that mean?

FIRST WOMAN. When the tale began it was night and when the caravan set on the journey it was night. They set on the journey from the East to the West. The tale changed its outfit at every place of accommodation. Every place they arrived, it was night. Since the narrator of the tales within the tale, Scheherazade, changed the night with words each time, the next day never came. Daylight never touched the tale. Stories postpone death. Time passed on the way. It passed through time. The night of the tale runs long. The East came to the West, always at night. That's why everywhere it went it was always night.

That's why the one thousand and one nights are indeed a single long night; it only lasts itself. From its own tale, it acquired a false truth that disintegrates when it sees daylight.

NARRATOR. Caravans carry not only tales, but also tools of performance from the East to the West—such as glass and tulle, bronze and silver, paper and silk. Like love, like love.

TEXT NARRATOR. Woman and Man enter the performance space, one from each side. Man, the moment he sees Woman, stands stunned, frozen in place. This is love. The tableau of the grip of love darkens the entire performance space. Man is unable to budge.

(*Silence.*)

The bells of the caravan call him, the time of the road calls, he wants to go, struggles, but cannot move. Woman goes behind the page. The page is smothered in light. She brings her face closer to the page. She becomes visible like a relief.

(*Silence.*)

Narrator joins the performance as a portraitist, moves to the front of the page, draws Woman's face on the page.

NARRATOR. In the past, they say, a lover would have a portrait drawn of their beloved so they could hold it against their chest. So as not to forget the face of the beloved and to look at it when in longing.

TEXT NARRATOR. When the portrait is complete, Narrator, as portraitist, retreats from between the page and Man. Then, Woman also retreats, her face remaining on the page. Her face is lost between the eyes of Man and the portrait on the page. That face is now only an emptiness whose original had been drawn on paper. The sound of the bells gets louder. The caravan embarks on the journey. On one of the pages is the caravan, on the other is the portrait. The lover embarks on the journey, following the portrait on the page. Once in a while, Woman enters between the portrait and the lover, obstructs the lover from seeing the portrait. She wants to make the lover look at her and not the portrait. The lover pushes Woman aside each time. He looks at the portrait. With the sound of the bells and the rhythm of the camels in the caravan accompanied by distant music, they cross the desert. Woman tries again to get behind the page, where her face is drawn. However, now she has been exiled from her own face. She is an image. Only an image. As she tries to find her face on the page, the page, turning on its axis, does not allow for anyone to settle on it.

NARRATOR. Love wanders far and wide. It is lost in its own desert.

(*Silence.*)

That is the region to which all the holy books have descended.

TEXT NARRATOR. When in love, time does not pass. When separated, time does not pass. The lover keeps shaking the hourglass, so time will pass faster. He wants to infect the sand, that is, time, with the fever he's caught. In the desert, time is measured with sand. However, sand only flows in its own time. The page with the drawing of the portrait ahead, Woman in-between, and the lover with the hourglass, shaking time in his hand, cross the performance space.

After this, each one passes the hourglass to someone else after turning it over once on their lap.

NARRATOR. Love is as it is on the page. Just as it is on the page.

The caravan crosses itself. The desert repeats itself. And the pages pour like the sand. To time and to each other.

TEXT NARRATOR. All the actors passionately read the pages of an invisible book in front of them, they voraciously turn the pages, they do what Narrator says.

NARRATOR. Those who want to get to the end of the tale very quickly wet their fingers each time with the tips of their tongues, as they swiftly turn the pages of a book which hides the secrets of life inside it. However, life goes on with the poisonous chemistry that was applied to the edges of the pages. Each page poisons its owner. No one can get to the end of the page. They die before the book ends. All is left half-done, as on the page. Life goes on with other pages, missing, half-done, incomplete, and desperately needing the lives of others. As they die, their heads fall onto each other's knees. They die as if falling asleep.

The first page that comes from the East finishes here.

The End

OLD WOMAN	Around 70, pretty spry but gives the impression she cannot walk in order to get attention.
OLD MAN	Around 80, can only walk with the help of his cane.
YOUNG WOMAN	Around 18, pregnant.
YOUNG MAN	Around 20.
MAN	Around 50.
WOMAN	Around 45.
MIDWIFE	Around 40.
PRESIDENT	Male, around 75.
FEMALE MEMBER	Around 60.
MALE MEMBER	Around 60.
GUARD 1	Around 35.
GUARD 2	Around 35.

AVALANCHE

TUNCER CÜCENOĞLU

NOTES ON THE PLAY

Avalanche premiered at the Akün Stage of Ankara State Theatre, Ankara, on November 20, 2007 with the following cast and crew:

Old Woman	Rengin Samurçay
Old Man	Nurtekin Odabaşı
Young Woman	Leyla Aykan Gülener
Young Man	Ötüken Hürmüzlü
Woman	Süheyla Gürkan
Man	Teoman Gülen
Midwife	Gül Gökçe
President	T. Tolga Tecer
Female Member	Oya Odabaşı
Male Member	Halit Güngör
Brother (*Image*)	Fikret Kuşkan
Ministers from Space	Öykü Başar, Ahmet Cem Şenoğlu
Dead Girl/Husband	Gamze Özlem Tezbaşaran
Head of Guards	Onur Uysal
Guard 1	Gürhan Altundaşar
Guard 2	Özgür Ertem
Guard 3	Vedat Kurtuluş Depe
Guard 4	Halis Işık
Women's Chorus	Gamze Özlem Tezbaşaran, Sevinç Yıldız, Emek Targan, Seçil Dedeyi, Sanem Gamze Gülşen, Gökçen Eroğlu, Furkan Çelebi, Deren Baybars

Director	Ayşe Emel Mesçi
Assistant Director	Gül Gökçe
Stage Designer	Murat Gülmez
Light Designer	Önder Arık
Costume Designer	Hale Eren
Original Music	Baba Zula
Poster Designer	Aydın Ayan
Mask Designer	İlhan Ateş
Coach for the Chorus	Semih Bayraktar
Movement Coach	Sevinç Yıldız
Assistants	Gamze Özlem Tezbaşaran, Emek Targan
Light Assistant	M. İlker Soyalp
Stage Manager	Kazım Kerimoğlu
Other Crew	Havva Evirgen, Ertuğrul Özkan, Özkan Özyürek, Burak Can, Latif Karagöz, Ali Eroğlu, Nejla Tekin, Rıfat Ağırtaş

SETTING A single-story house in a small settlement surrounded by mountains. Icicles can be seen through the windows. Two rifles are mounted on the back wall. The barrels face each other, the stocks apart. They have been hung almost aesthetically.

There's a room on the left. There's a large common room in the middle. On the right is a door that opens to another room. The outside door is opposite that. In the common space is a primitive fireplace. Next to the fireplace is a neatly stacked woodpile. There are rugs on the floor and small, tapestry-like carpets hang on the walls.

There's also a drum and its timpani mallet in a corner of the living room. It's as if they're waiting for the day when they can sound out.

In the room on the left side, Young Woman and Young Man are sleeping.

In the living room, Old Woman lies near the fireplace, looking at the ceiling. She abides in a state between sleeping and waking. Next to her, her husband, Old Man, is sleeping like the dead. He is almost unnoticeable. In the room on the right, Man and Woman are sleeping. Everyone is on mattresses on the floor.

The sections of the house are not partitioned with walls. The space is not realistic but symbolic.

Utter silence abounds. This silence will last throughout the performance, until the end. Place changes and other movements should be silent. Actions are measured, almost like a slow-motion movie. The dialogue should be stage-whispered until the end. The audience should be made to sense that the characters are careful not to talk loudly, not to make noise, and gradually, that the characters are afraid.

AVALANCHE
Tuncer Cücenoğlu

ACT I

The day breaks slowly. There's neither the sound of a dog's bark, nor a rooster's crow. Utter silence reigns. As the day breaks, an incredible white glare enters the space. The silence seems to grow with the dawn.

Old Woman is the first to get up. First, she makes sure that everyone else is asleep, then quietly, she goes into the bathroom. She comes back a little later, picks something up from the kitchen area and quickly puts it into her mouth, looking around to make sure that she won't get caught.

Young Woman sits up in bed with a grimace. It's obvious that she is experiencing abdominal pain. She hesitates for a moment, not sure whether or not to wake her husband. She decides against waking him and quietly gets up. It's obvious that she's pregnant.

Old Woman, sensing that Young Woman is approaching, gets back into her bed, her mouth still full. She pretends to be asleep. In fact, in order to make Young Woman pity her, she pushes the bedcovers off herself.

Young Woman, walking quietly, first enters the living room, then the bathroom. Old Woman's gaze follows Young Woman.

Young Woman returns to the living room a little later, looking relieved. She walks with the same care as before. She goes to Old Woman's sleeping area. She covers Old Woman, thinking that she is asleep. As Young Woman goes back to her room, Old Woman is happy to have succeeded, and keeps chewing the food in her mouth. Young Woman gets in bed.

This time Young Man gets up and leaves the room. He passes through the common area and goes outside. Old Woman pretends to be asleep. Knowing that Young Man will return, she again pushes the blanket off.

Young Man comes back a little later. He covers up Old Woman then goes to his room, gets in bed.

Old Woman opens her eyes, blinks; she is left alone with her thoughts, fitfully turning her head from side to side.

Young Woman suddenly sits up. Clearly, the pain has returned.

YOUNG WOMAN (*poking Young Man*). Get up.

YOUNG MAN (*groggily*). What's up?

YOUNG WOMAN. My stomach.

YOUNG MAN. What about it?

YOUNG WOMAN. I'm in pain.

YOUNG MAN. Go to the bathroom.

YOUNG WOMAN. I have.

YOUNG MAN. And?

YOUNG WOMAN. It came back. I'm scared.

YOUNG MAN (*disbelieving*). What is there to be scared of?

YOUNG WOMAN. What do you mean, "what is there?"

YOUNG MAN. You're probably sick. (*He is worried nevertheless.*) What else could it be? (*Silence.*) How are you now?

YOUNG WOMAN. It passed.

YOUNG MAN. There's nothing to be scared of.

YOUNG WOMAN. For a moment I thought that was it.

YOUNG MAN. What?

YOUNG WOMAN. I thought it was labor pains.

YOUNG MAN. That doesn't make sense.

YOUNG WOMAN. What was it, then?

YOUNG MAN. You're confusing gas pain with labor pain.

YOUNG WOMAN. It kicked. The baby is kicking.

YOUNG MAN (*putting his hand on Young Woman's belly, smiling happily*). That's wonderful. It seems it's getting impatient.

YOUNG WOMAN. It needs to be patient for a few more days.

YOUNG MAN (*taking Young Woman's hand*). Put these fears out of your mind. You have at least a month. There's nothing to be afraid of. There has never been an untimely birth around here. Didn't my grandmother tell you that?

YOUNG WOMAN. But there *have* been untimely births.

YOUNG MAN. Who did you hear that from?

YOUNG WOMAN. From your grandmother.

YOUNG MAN. But that was a long time ago.

YOUNG WOMAN. What difference does that make?

YOUNG MAN (*dismissively*). That was before we were born.

YOUNG WOMAN. They put the pregnant woman in a coffin while she was still alive.

YOUNG MAN. She told you that?

YOUNG WOMAN. She was telling your mother. I heard.

YOUNG MAN. That was in the past. Nothing like that has happened since then. Go back to sleep!

Young Woman closes her eyes, trying to fall asleep. This time it's Young Man's turn to be uneasy. He caresses his wife's hair. He is pensive.

The whiteness outside has reached its peak. However, the incredible silence is still building gradually.

YOUNG WOMAN (*opening her eyes*). What if I had really gone into labor?

YOUNG MAN. It won't happen.

YOUNG WOMAN. Why?

YOUNG MAN. Because the elders have everything figured out.

YOUNG WOMAN. And they're never wrong?

YOUNG MAN. No!

YOUNG WOMAN. Why?

YOUNG MAN. Because mistakes will affect them as well.

Silence.

YOUNG WOMAN. But . . . You were scared, too.

YOUNG MAN. Isn't that natural?

YOUNG WOMAN. Then my fear is natural, too.

YOUNG MAN. I didn't say it wasn't. But that's not the case. Anyway, if it happens two days from now, there will be no danger. Our horses, donkeys, dogs, cows, sheep, roosters, and even the chickens, will be brought back. Even if it's only for three months. Then, you will give birth like rifles fired into the air. Our baby will let out its first cry. It won't scare us. It will cry countless times! The others won't be afraid either. Because it won't be dangerous anymore. (*Starts caressing Young Woman's hair.*) Everyone will sing songs. Even the oldest will be drunk as a lord and dance in the town square. For exactly three months! This will go on for three months. Then when the first snow falls, you and I will take our baby, climb over the mountains, go away from here. So that we can raise our child without fear. Those who will have returned with their animals will leave the same way. Because horses neigh, donkeys bray, dogs bark, cows moo, roosters crow, and hens cluck. Should I tell you a secret?

YOUNG WOMAN. Tell.

YOUNG MAN. We'll never come back. Just like the kids who have already left. We'll leave and we'll live to our heart's content. Without fear. Until we feel that death is close, only then will we come back here. Just like our elders.

YOUNG WOMAN. We won't come back? Not even when summer comes?

YOUNG MAN. Not you and our son, but I will come, because we have to bring food for the ones who stay here for the winter. What would all these people do without flour, sugar, and salt?

YOUNG WOMAN. You said "you and our son." How do you know we'll have a son? Maybe we'll have a daughter.

YOUNG MAN. Maybe. I was just saying it, so to speak.

YOUNG WOMAN. But I will want to see my parents, too, I couldn't stand the longing.

YOUNG MAN. What's keeping them here? They can come with us.

YOUNG WOMAN. Then your parents should come, too. If we all go, even if it's temporary, you won't have to come back.

YOUNG MAN. Mine won't come, because my grandfather and grandmother came here to die. Forget about my parents. Let's think about our child. Our child should grow up without fear. (*He does not realize that Young Woman has fallen asleep.*) A wise old man once said these exact words: "In the presence of fear, a person can't develop the capacity for thought. Fear is the most negative influence, distorting and twisting the thinking of man. Don't let your children live in fear!" No, no. I can't let that happen. (*Realizes that Young Woman has fallen asleep. He leaves her side quietly, goes to the common area. Old Woman pretends to be asleep again. To Old Woman*) I know you're not asleep, Grandmother.

OLD WOMAN. What's up, son?

YOUNG MAN. I need to ask you something.

OLD WOMAN. Go on.

YOUNG MAN. You were talking to Mother the other day. You mentioned someone who went into labor early. A long time ago.

OLD WOMAN (*suspiciously*). Why are you asking about that?

YOUNG MAN. My wife is very scared.

OLD WOMAN. Why is she scared? She doesn't have that problem.

YOUNG MAN. No, she doesn't. But she's scared. She's young and impressionable. It got to her. Besides, I'm curious.

OLD WOMAN (*getting a kick out of it*). At the time, I was young, like your wife. I was one of the young brides. We all got married at a splendid wedding. But our wedding night had to wait for at least four months. The elders told us. Three of us managed to stay away from our partners. But one didn't. She started seeing her husband every night. And then? She went into labor three months before the threat of the avalanche had passed. And then whatever happened, happened.

YOUNG MAN. What happened?

OLD WOMAN. The rules are clear. The midwife was called immediately. Everything was in order. The council convened and took the decision we all knew it would. Our friend was put in a coffin and buried in one of the graves that had been prepared earlier.

YOUNG MAN. What did her husband do?

OLD WOMAN. He wept a lot. He begged them to stop. He pleaded. He asked the council to bury him, too. But they told him nothing could be done. And they rejected his request to be buried with his wife.

YOUNG MAN. And then?

OLD WOMAN. When the threat of the avalanches had passed, the coffin was opened. Three months later. By then, there was nothing we could do for our friend.

YOUNG MAN. That's cruel.

OLD WOMAN. It was necessary for everyone's survival. They couldn't endanger other lives knowing that an avalanche would hit! What else could be done?

YOUNG MAN. How would I know? Maybe the woman could have been gagged during labor. That way they could have prevented her from crying out.

OLD WOMAN. You know it's forbidden to think like that. It was so in the past, it is now. But us women, without letting anyone hear, have tried that among ourselves. But when? Once the danger had passed, when we were giving birth one after the other, we all tried to keep silent as though an avalanche could occur . . . the screams were unbelievable. They echoed through the hills. As if they were calling the avalanche upon us. Even a baby's cry could bring all of our deaths. Don't forget, even the most cruel rules are in place for human happiness.

YOUNG MAN. What kind of happiness is this? What kind of conscience can explain how burying someone alive can bring happiness?

OLD WOMAN. Who put these thoughts in your head? Don't worry about this. What's done is done. They say one incident is better than a thousand admonishments. Maybe that death is why it hasn't happened again in the last fifty years.

IMAGE 2.2 **Women executed for giving birth early.**
Ötüken Hürmüzlü as Young Man and Leyla Aykan Gülener as Young Woman.
Avalanche, Akün Stage, Ankara State Theater, Ankara, 2007.
Photograph by Muzaffer Aykanat (Courtesy: Ankara State Theater).

Young Man is silent for a while, then goes to the bathroom. In the next room, Woman wakes up and silently leaves the bed. Trying not to wake Man, she leaves the room as if she is gliding. She looks Old Woman in the eye.

OLD WOMAN (*pointing toward the bathroom*). Your son is in there.

WOMAN. What woke you?

OLD WOMAN. I got hungry.

WOMAN (*pretending not to hear*). Go back to sleep!

Man gets up, silently comes over.

OLD WOMAN (*sees that Man has come but pretends not to notice*). I got hungry, I said. I'm hungry!

WOMAN. You expect a lot from me.

OLD WOMAN. If I could stand, would I ask you?

WOMAN (*prepares some food, places it in front of Old Woman*). Don't drop any on the bed!

OLD WOMAN. When did I ever drop any on the bed?

WOMAN. I didn't say you have. I said don't!

OLD WOMAN. If I've never dropped any, why do you say "don't drop any?" Clearly I'm careful.

WOMAN. You're hassling me for no reason!

OLD WOMAN. I wouldn't hassle you if you didn't ask for it . . .

WOMAN. All right, hassle away then.

OLD WOMAN. This is too dry to eat!

WOMAN. What do you want now, tea?

OLD WOMAN. A little water would be enough!

Man has patiently listened to the conversation. He gives a scolding look to Woman.

MAN (*to Woman*). We have a lot of work to do. We need to get prepared.

WOMAN. Were you here the whole time?

MAN. Wake everyone up.

WOMAN (*more quietly*). If I have any time left after dealing with your mother!

Old Woman tells Man with gestures that Young Man has left the toilet.

OLD WOMAN. Water!

Grumbling, Woman gives her water, then walks to the fireplace, and silently stirs the embers. The fire flares up a bit. She then adds more water to the kettle over the fire.

Man approaches and caresses Old Woman's cheek. With her eyes, Old Woman complains about Woman.

Man is used to it; he gestures "please put up with it."

Young Man comes. Man gestures to Young Man for his daughter-in-law to be woken up too.

Young Man nods, goes in to their room. Bending over, he strokes Young Woman's hair. Young Woman takes Young Man's hand. The couple lingers in the pleasant moment.

YOUNG MAN. How are you now?

YOUNG WOMAN. Fine.

YOUNG MAN. I told you so. (*Silence.*) There's much work to do. It would be best if you got up now.

Young Woman gets up. Silently, she makes the bed. She and Young Man, who has been waiting, go to the living room. While Woman and Young Woman set the eating area on the floor, Man and Young Man bring down the rifles from the wall.

Man starts cleaning one of them with a cloth from a bag Young Man has brought. He demonstrates it step-by-step to Young Man.

Young Man cleans the other rifle just like Man.

Woman and Young Woman prepare and tidy up the dining area, moving as though in slow motion. By now, both rifles are clean.

The teacups are filled.

When Young Man wants to load the rifle he has cleaned, Man grimaces and stops him.

MAN. Not now. It's not time yet.

YOUNG MAN. I wonder, how is the water in the trough doing?

MAN (*demonstrating with his hand*). There were three fingers of space left.

They return the rifles to the wall. As the women continue setting the table, Young Man puts the box of bullets close to the rifles, then pours water onto Man's hands, allowing him to wash his face. Man dries his face with a towel.

YOUNG MAN. Should I check the trough?

MAN. Go ahead, if you feel like it.

Young Man leaves silently. The women finish setting the table.

YOUNG MAN (*enters; demonstrates with his hand*). About two and a half fingers.

MAN. Good. Maybe it will fill up today and we'll be able to fire the rifles. But it will be full by tomorrow at the latest.

YOUNG MAN. Hopefully! As long as it's not late!

MAN. Why the rush? As long as it fills up, let it be late a couple of days! No one's chasing us!

Man sits first. Then the others.

MAN. Why didn't you wake my father?

OLD WOMAN. Let us eat in peace. I'll feed him later. This way he won't bother us. Do you have any idea the kind of man he was? He would not sit in one place. The old folks say you should see the wolf when he gets old. Well, this is what happens to the wolf when he gets old.

WOMAN. May all our friends age so well. He can take care of all his needs.

OLD WOMAN. (*She smiles bitterly.*) That's what you think!

Everyone drinks tea, careful to be silent. They eat. When the teacups are empty, Young Woman refills them.

When the food in front of her is gone, Old Woman asks Man for more with a poke. Sometimes she pokes Young Man. But she is always wary of Woman. Suddenly Old Man sits up in bed.

He looks at those having breakfast without comprehension.

OLD WOMAN. Come here. (*To the others*) Make room, let him approach. Why don't you come closer? (*She pulls him with her hand, tries to bring him closer to the table.*) Why don't you come closer? (*Man also helps. Old Woman tries to stuff some food into Old Man's mouth, as though it is some bitter medicine. Old Woman raises her hands in prayer and continues*). My God! Don't let me this happen to me! When the day comes, take me silently.

OLD MAN (*softer than others, almost inaudible*). Everyone left. I left, too.

MAN. Dad, eat your food.

OLD MAN. The young all left and never came back. But what did we do? We came back. We came back at the end of every winter. We came back with all the flour, sugar, salt, barley, and wheat that we worked for and bought. So that all these people could eat during the winter. Every year, we taught you to be a bit quieter and we came back. Now we're here for good. That's why it's my right to fire the rifle first. It's my right every year. It's my right this year. It will always be my right.

MAN. Eat your food, Dad.

OLD MAN. The brave man is the one who raises his baby and comes back. The brave man is the one who comes back knowing the joy of shouting. Is there anyone who has a word to say about my bravery? (*Silence.*) When will we fire the rifles?

MAN. Maybe tomorrow, Dad.

OLD MAN. They look down on me. They say I have come back to my land like the elephants who are close to death.

MAN. Let them say what they want, Dad. Those who know, know. You came back here because you love your land.

OLD MAN (*sobs*). The truth is I don't know why I came back anymore. (*He sobs again.*) I no longer take pleasure in eating, or drinking, or anything else. Not even firing the rifles. Your bird doesn't sing, your teeth can't chew! Is this life?

OLD WOMAN (*to herself*) Your teeth have always been able to chew! Your bird has never shut up! It's a wash! (*To Old Man*) Come on, stop talking crazy and eat!

WOMAN (*very quietly*). I'm sick of this! I've had enough!

OLD MAN. Friend! If you're alive, your bird must be singing! Your teeth must be able to chew! Only then would I say that a person is alive.

OLD WOMAN. We've seen the days when your bird was singing! Everyone but I enjoyed it! What did it get me?

OLD MAN. It doesn't get you anything if you don't appreciate it.

OLD WOMAN. If you try to make the bird sing for every meal, of course there's no hunger left! If you eat the same thing every day, you'll get sick of it, too, even if it's honey!

OLD MAN. Others would cause it to sing! Look for the blame in yourself a little bit!

OLD WOMAN. I guess you won't shut up about this. Now that I've seen what happens when your bird doesn't sing, I won't grieve anymore! (*Angrily*) Drink your tea! You don't need teeth to drink tea! Even without teeth, stuff goes down to your stomach. (*Quietly*) But if your bird can't fly, why bother!

OLD MAN (*ornery*). For God's sake, woman! Stay out of my business.

OLD WOMAN. Fine. Wallow in self-pity! Cry! Cry! It will relax you, cry!

As Old Man quietly weeps, the others continue having breakfast. By now the room is bright, almost as if the sun is in the house.

Old Man drinks his tea, finishes his breakfast, then gets up and goes to the bathroom.

Woman and Young Woman start clearing the table.

Old Man returns and sits down.

As Young Woman quietly washes the dishes in the kitchen area, Old Man signals Woman to give him a cigarette.

MAN. Give him one!

Woman takes a cigarette from a hiding place and hands it to Old Man. Old Man takes the cigarette happily. He gestures to Man to light it. Man does so.

OLD MAN (*joyfully takes a drag from the cigarette and loses himself for a moment. To Man*). You never met your uncle. If he was still alive, he would be by my side now. He was two years older than me. An introverted child. He never talked. We were all scared that there would be some noise and an avalanche would fall. but he was more afraid. (*He gestures, indicating the room.*) We used to sleep side by side. Sometimes he would have nightmares. He would wake up, sweating bullets. I would ask him what happened in his nightmares. He would never answer. Then one day, after I promised I wouldn't tell anyone, he told me his fears. He spoke of how he felt with his entire being that, any second, it would all end with a bang. "It doesn't matter how careful you are. What if someone else makes a mistake? One second we're here, and then, boom, we're gone. There's nothing we can do. My God, it's terrible to be helpless!" He was scared, he spent his whole life worrying that an avalanche would happen. Fear consumes a person. It eats them up. Fear is a parasite. Another time, after another nightmare, he said: "I want to go outside and scream. I can't help myself." "Are you crazy?" I said, "There'll be an avalanche. We'll all die. Didn't you say you were afraid of that?" "Death comes whether we fear it or not," he replied. "I'm sick of being afraid. I have no other way to face my fear! It's better to die, to stop being afraid than to live in constant fear. One day I'll scream at the top of my lungs. Then I'll have conquered my fear! I want to scream!" "OK," I said, "You'll have saved us from our fear as well." I said this but after I got really scared. What if he had taken me seriously and screamed? (*Suddenly falls asleep.*)

Man picks up Old Man's ashtray and puts it away. As Young Woman washes the dishes, she totters, then grimaces in pain. Young Man, mindful of her earlier pain, approaches her.

YOUNG MAN (*quietly*). What is it?

YOUNG WOMAN. It started again.

YOUNG MAN. It will pass.

YOUNG WOMAN. I can't take it. (*She moans.*) I can't take it.

YOUNG MAN. You have to!

YOUNG WOMAN. It's out of my hands.

YOUNG MAN. Be patient!

Old Woman is suspicious. She watches the two of them. But she still doesn't entirely understand the situation.

YOUNG WOMAN. What can I do?

YOUNG MAN. Don't let on!

YOUNG WOMAN. How?

YOUNG MAN. Let's go to our room.

IMAGE 2.3 **Young Woman's pain.**
Leyla Aykan Gülener as Young Woman and Ötüken Hürmüzlü as Young Man. *Avalanche*, Akün Stage, Ankara State Theater, Ankara, 2007.
Photograph by Muzaffer Aykanat (Courtesy: Ankara State Theater).

Young Woman and Young Man slowly head to the room. They move quietly, as though nothing is wrong. Young Woman is still in pain.

YOUNG MAN. How is it now?

YOUNG WOMAN. The same.

YOUNG MAN. It will pass.

YOUNG WOMAN. I think our fear has come true. I've never felt pain like this. It can only be labor! (*She begins to cry quietly.*) What will happen now? What will we do?

IMAGE 2.4 **Young Woman in labor.**
Ötüken Hürmüzlü as Young Man and Leyla Aykan Gülener as Young Woman. *Avalanche*, Akün Stage, Ankara State Theater, Ankara, 2007.
Photograph by Muzaffer Aykanat (Courtesy: Ankara State Theater).

YOUNG MAN (*helpless but hopeful*). It's not labor! You're not due yet! Our first time together was around New Year's Eve. It hasn't been nine months. (*He counts on his fingers.*) There's at least a month until the birth. It will pass. Don't be so pessimistic!

Woman notices the absence of Young Woman. Then looks at the dishes. Thinking Young Woman has left the dishes for her, she gets angry and begins washing them.

Man is carving pieces of wood.

Old Woman is trying to understand what's happening. Old Man is sleeping deeply. Snoring gently. Woman finishes washing up.

WOMAN (*drying her hands*). Have you seen the young woman?

MAN. They went to their room. Why did you ask?

WOMAN. She left without washing the dishes.

MAN. Don't lay too much on the girl. Her labor is near.

WOMAN. I wish I'd had a father-in-law like you. There was no one thinking of me like this.

MAN. Don't worry about the past.

WOMAN. When it's about me, you say "don't worry!" But now I'm taking care of them. Both of them.

MAN. And you'll keep doing it! That's your job. And our children will take care of us.

WOMAN. I'm surprised that you expect that from the kids of today. What makes you think they'll come back? Watch what happens when they have their baby. Once they're gone, you think they'll ever come back? Has anyone from their generation come back?

MAN. My child is different. He will.

WOMAN. Your child will want to come back, but will your daughter-in-law allow it? Look, your son hangs on her every word. As if she's the first woman to get pregnant.

Old Woman senses that Man and Woman are arguing. She tries to listen but can't. At the same time, she tries to look at the young couple inside.

MAN. Don't you start being a mother-in-law again!

WOMAN. When I tell the truth, you call it "being a mother-in-law."

MAN. You're dragging it out. We both know what kind of daughter-in-law you were. I remember how you treated my mom. You're still torturing the poor woman.

Silence. Young Woman's pain has stopped. Young Man wipes beads of sweat off her face.

YOUNG MAN. See? It passed.

YOUNG WOMAN. I hope so.

YOUNG MAN. Let's go back. So they don't get suspicious.

Young Man and Young Woman go into the main area. Old Woman still hasn't figured out what's going on, but she's obviously trying. Young Woman walks to the kitchen area.

WOMAN (*sarcastically*). Don't bother, daughter. I washed them.

YOUNG MAN. She got dizzy, Mom.

Young Man sits beside Man. He picks up a piece of wood, starts carving. He finishes it. He puts it by the other ones he's finished, and starts another one. Young Woman covers up Old Man. She stirs the fire.

OLD WOMAN (*timidly*). Son, can you take me to the . . .

Man and Young Man get up immediately. Clearly, they don't know that Old Woman can walk. They each take one of Old Woman's arms and help her slowly to the toilet.

WOMAN (*gets up and closes the door behind them*). Wretched thing!

YOUNG WOMAN. At least she asks, Mother. What would we do if she didn't?

WOMAN (*angrily*). What would we do? What could we do? We put up with it. I wouldn't mind it as much if I had someone saying "let me help with the work!"

YOUNG WOMAN. I'm sorry, Mother. I have become quite big. Still, I try to help as much as I can.

Woman doesn't respond. Man and Young Man bring back Old Woman, almost as though they're driving her. They put her in her bed.

OLD WOMAN. May God bless you! May all that you touch turn to gold! May God give you all that you wish! May God give you a healthy lad like a ray of light!

YOUNG MAN. Hopefully, Grandma. When the time is right. That way we'll have nothing to fear!

Man and Young Man pick up pieces of wood again. They continue carving. Old Woman appears to be about to sneeze. She covers her mouth and nose and sneezes quietly.

THE OTHERS. God bless you!

OLD WOMAN. You too!

OLD MAN (*suddenly wakes up, continues to tell the story about his brother from where he left off*). I said, "No! You can't do this! You can't scream! If you do, we'll all die! Doesn't it bother you that we'll all die?" "It does but I can't help myself. I want to go out and scream in the doorway." I could tell that he was sorry as he was saying this because he was crying. He was moaning, "If it goes on like this, I will cause all of your deaths. Dear God, what kind of passion is this! I don't think anyone has ever wanted to scream so much. This is the same as wanting a woman. I want to scream with all my being. I can't give up this thought. I can't help myself." I was in a difficult situation. Because everyone feared the avalanche. But my fear was that, one day, my brother would scream. And that was fear of the avalanche, too. I watched my brother constantly. Even in the bathroom I was after him. I always looked into his eyes, silently pleading. Sometimes he would make a fist and open his mouth, but when he saw my eyes he would suppress his need to scream, clenching his teeth. Then one day he said, "I don't want to scream anymore!" "For real?" "Yes," he said. I can't express how happy I was. I couldn't hold my tears back. Before I could say, "My brother is getting better," he kept on talking. "How much can I scream? Screaming won't satiate me. I will fire the rifle. Yes, yes, I will fire the rifle! Because when I fire the rifle, these mountains will come down on us like nothing else!" Dear God. My brother was really losing his mind. I went to Dad and explained the situation. "That's good!" said Dad. "If we hide the bullets, nothing will happen." "But," I said, "what if he gets angry? If he can't fire the rifle he'll get angry and then he will scream. You don't need to fire a rifle for an avalanche to happen, Dad. A strong scream is enough to end it all. He's made up his mind. He'll make the avalanche fall on us. You're still trying to hide from the truth in order to protect him! But I'm your son, too! I will die. So will you. And if we don't say anything we'll be as guilty as him. Even if we escape the avalanche. You need to accept this now, Dad. He has gone insane. If we don't say something and make them take precautions, and God forbid, he does scream, what will we do? When the avalanche hits, can either of us outrun it? Can we afford mercy? Can we watch everyone die out of pity for one person? You have to report this even though he's your son, Dad!" My father began to think seriously for the first time. He couldn't deny it any longer. "You're right!" he said. He went and reported the situation to the Elders. They listened quietly. They gave no response for a long time. This was the first time such a situation had arisen. "What will you do to my son?" Dad asked, "I have a right to know." After deliberating, the judges said, "Citizen, what choice do we have? It's clear what we must do. Obviously we're not going to just wait for death! We gag him, bind his hands and feet and put him in a corner." "For how long?" "Until the threat of the avalanche passes. How can we trust someone who has gone insane? What if he screams?" But my father had a point: "How can a person live without drinking or eating? You're condemning him to death, and you know it." But they weren't even listening. Immediately, they tied my brother's hands and feet, gagged him and laid him down in the common house. Once in a while the guards fed him. In order to stop him from screaming during the meals, they would stuff food into his mouth, then clamp their huge hands immediately over it. This lasted for fifteen days. Easier said than done, fifteen days. Then one day they came and said, 'Your son is dead!' We never learned if he died on his own, or if the guards suffocated him. (*He falls asleep.*)

MAN (*to Young Man*). Do you know that story?

YOUNG MAN. How could I not know?

WOMAN. God knows how many times we've heard it!

YOUNG WOMAN. Even I've heard it at least three times.

OLD WOMAN. The first time I gave birth, after the danger of the ava-lanche had passed, (*to Man*) you were born. When the first snow fell, we left. After we arrived, we were quiet like this for a long time. We stayed in an immigrant neighborhood with others who migrated from here. Our customs continued. We were quiet and timid. The locals liked us a lot. They wanted us to do every job. Because we never said no, we never reacted. We'd take whatever was offered, we didn't begrudge what was not. Come, come. Go, go. Give, give. We did the hardest jobs. The locals were very different. Noisy, belligerent. They could laugh out loud. They liked us a lot but they wouldn't let us talk about this place. "We accepted you. What else do you want? Just work! We can't allow negativity!" Then I had my second child. Another boy. But he didn't live. Then we had a daughter. She didn't live either. Your father began to change. Apparently, he was sad about his brother. He'd come home drunk every night. "This suffering will kill me!" he'd say. I believed it. Then I learned he was seeing another woman. When I asked, "Why are you seeing her?" he said, "How should I know why the pain of the loss of my brother makes me do what I do? Let me be!" "Let me be!" he'd say, over and over, and visit all the women in the area. His excuse was that he could not endure the loss of his brother. "Let me distract myself! Or this pain will kill me," he'd say. How frightfully good women can be at easing a man's suffering! I learned that from my husband. There was a neighbor, an old woman. She knew what a womanizer he was. One day she came home and said to me, "There are many ways to make a man come home! Instead of crying and moaning, take care of yourself and welcome your husband with a smile!" I did what she said, but he didn't even see me. Then she advised that I cook his favorite foods. But he didn't eat when he came home, even the foods he liked the most. Because he came home full. Completely drunk and full—I also learned from my husband how hard it is to feed the full. Finally, our neighbor recommended a third way. The child and I would be ill from time to time. I learned that with illness one can gather the attention of people, especially husbands. "Just the illness of the child isn't enough. You should be ill, too, so he doesn't hope that you will take care of the kid!" I followed her recommendation and managed to make my husband come home. But at what cost! Don't be fooled by how he is sleeping now! He made me suffer a lot!

Suddenly Young Woman starts writhing in pain. She doubles over. With great effort, she goes to the other room. Young Man notices and follows—he'd been watching her.

Old Woman also sees notices happening. Frightened, she tries to figure it out.

YOUNG WOMAN. I can't stand it! Dear God! I can't stand it!

YOUNG MAN. What can I do? Have patience!

YOUNG WOMAN. This is labor, get it? Dear God! Do something! Save me!

Old Woman tries to tell Man something. When Man doesn't understand, she gets up, agitated, and walks to him. When Woman sees Old Woman walking, she is astounded, almost speechless.

OLD WOMAN. Son! Daughter!

MAN. What is it, Mom?

WOMAN. Your mother can walk!

MAN. Mom! You're walking!

OLD WOMAN. Am I walking? Yes, yes, I'm walking. Forget about that right now. She's going into labor!

MAN. What are you talking about, Mom?

WOMAN. Your mother can walk!

MAN. Didn't you hear what she said? She says the baby's coming!

All three go to the next room. For a while they watch, aghast. The others are not aware of their presence.

Young Man repeatedly signals Young Woman to be quiet. Young Woman, on the other hand, is writhing in pain.

MAN. What's going on, son?

WOMAN. Did something happen?

YOUNG MAN. It's nothing.

WOMAN. Look.

YOUNG WOMAN. My stomach hurts. (*She tries to hide it.*) It will pass soon.

They're all watching Young Woman. She struggles to hide her pain but she can't endure it any longer and collapses on the floor.

WOMAN. It's happening! Oh my God!

YOUNG MAN. It's not, Mom. It's only a stomachache.

WOMAN. Hopefully. Would you like some water?

YOUNG WOMAN. I can't take it anymore. (*She starts to moan.*)

YOUNG MAN (*covers Young Woman's mouth with his hand*). It will pass soon.

WOMAN. No, it won't.

MAN. What's happening?

YOUNG MAN. Her stomach hurts, Dad.

WOMAN. This doesn't look like a stomachache. I have given birth enough times. This is labor. Labor!

MAN. Oh, dear God!

OLD WOMAN. I told you so!

WOMAN. What will happen now?

Young Woman's pain passes. She relaxes. But her face is beaded with sweat.

YOUNG MAN. I told you it would pass. Look, it has.

WOMAN. It hasn't. This is just a break. It will come back soon.

MAN. How do you know?

WOMAN. Who knows better than me? I gave birth six times, even if most of them didn't survive. Let's be clear, this is labor.

Silence for a while.

MAN. We have to be sure.

YOUNG WOMAN. It's gone. I had a stomachache, but it's gone.

OLD WOMAN. It's always like this. First there's pain, then it passes. Then there will be pain again, and it will pass again. And then . . .

YOUNG MAN. How?

MAN (*decided*). Go, call the midwife.

YOUNG MAN. But . . .

MAN. We have to call her. If this isn't labor, then there's no problem. This way we can all relax. It's better to be awake then sleep in fear.

YOUNG MAN. What if it's labor?

MAN. Call her.

YOUNG MAN. What if it's labor?

WOMAN. Then we will have done what we're supposed to do. There's nothing else we can do. We have to call the midwife.

They are quiet for a little longer.

MAN. We can't take the responsibility anymore. Each passing second counts. We have to follow the rules.

YOUNG MAN. But—

MAN (*decisively*). We can't endanger other lives. We can't forget that we have to report possible risks. We know the rules. We can't act like as if we don't. Call the midwife.

YOUNG MAN. No!

MAN. We have to call her!

YOUNG MAN. This isn't labor! It happened before and it went away when she went to the bathroom. It's nothing. She's fine now! Let's wait a little longer.

MAN. What will we wait for? For her to give birth?

YOUNG MAN. She won't give birth!

MAN. How do you know? We have to be sure. I said call!

YOUNG MAN. Mom, stop! Let's not panic when there's no need. Wait!

MAN. What will she wait for? You're making us waste time! Don't waste time! Go and call her!

YOUNG WOMAN. Wait, Mother! Look, it passed! It passed. I'm fine! I swear this isn't labor!

OLD WOMAN. Daughter, if it's not labor, why are you afraid? The midwife will decide, then we can relax. Right, my child?

MAN. My mother is telling the truth. We have to be sure. Only the midwife can tell us that.

YOUNG MAN. What if it's labor?

WOMAN. We answered that! Didn't we? Won't we be punished because we didn't report this immediately? Don't you know the biggest crime is to hide a situation like this?

MAN. (*decided*). We have to be sure. Did you sleep together before the right day?

YOUNG MAN. Dad, how could you think I'd be so irresponsible?

MAN. Then why are you trying to stop the midwife from coming? Tell me, why? Why don't you tell me? Tell me! I told you to tell me! Tell me! Tell! Aren't you listening to me? Tell me!

Man gets close to Young Man and tries to vent his anger by squeezing the latter's hand and arm.

YOUNG MAN. It's not what you think, Dad! I swear it's not!

MAN. Then why are you scared, you asshole! (*He continues to squeeze.*) You will destroy this family's honor. You couldn't wait a month! Would this have happened if you could keep it in your pants? How can we go out in public now? We'll be the family who can't keep it in their pants! Have you no shame?

You have endangered everyone with your impatience. My reputation will be worthless! Because of you we'll be remembered as the family who endangered everyone! People will avoid us. They won't trust us! They'll ostracize us!

YOUNG MAN. I'm telling you, I didn't do it, Dad!

YOUNG WOMAN (*cries*). We didn't do it, Father! We didn't do anything to upset you!

Man hesitates, realizing that he's gone too far.

WOMAN (*eases Man's grip*). He says he didn't do it. Let him be.

Man lets go of Young Man. He relaxes for a while, calms down.

MAN (*still decided*). We have to be sure. Go call the midwife. Come on, don't stop! Don't lose time! Quick!

WOMAN. What should I say?

MAN (*stops, thinks for a moment*). You will say, "We're worried about our daughter-in-law. You'd better see her. We want to be sure." But don't forget to say that the pain has just started. They mustn't think we wasted time!

Woman puts on a headscarf and quietly goes out into the street. Young Woman cries helplessly. She puts on headphones and listens to a moving song. The others wait anxiously.

Curtain.

ACT II

Young Woman, sad and worried, sits in her room. Young Man sits nearby, thinking, apparently searching for a solution. Old Woman sits in her place, waiting, her eyes on the door. Man waits inside the house, looking through the window once in a while. Old Man is sleeping. The front door opens and Woman enters.

MAN. What happened?

WOMAN. I told her.

MAN. What did she say?

WOMAN. She's on her way.

MAN. Why didn't she come with you?

WOMAN. Apparently she has to report it to the guards first.

Woman goes to Young Woman's side. Woman hesitates for a moment, then strokes her hair to console her.

YOUNG WOMAN. Is she here ?

WOMAN. She will be. Did anything happen while I was gone?

YOUNG WOMAN. No!

WOMAN. I hope what we fear won't happen.

YOUNG WOMAN. Hopefully.

WOMAN. Maybe it's not labor.

YOUNG WOMAN. Hopefully.

WOMAN. You're not angry with me, are you?

YOUNG WOMAN. Do I have a right to be angry?

WOMAN. What choice do we have? We had to let them know as soon as possible. Me or someone else, it wouldn't have mattered. Someone had to let them know.

YOUNG WOMAN. I know.

Silence.

YOUNG WOMAN. I'm scared.

WOMAN. There's nothing we can do!

YOUNG WOMAN. I'm very scared.

Through the window, Man sees Midwife coming. He becomes flustered and goes over to Woman.

MAN. They're coming!

Man and Woman open the door.

WOMAN. Welcome!

MAN. Come in.

Midwife enters, followed by Guard 1.

MIDWIFE. Good morning.

GUARD 1. Morning.

MAN. Good morning.

YOUNG MAN. Good morning.

WOMAN. You, too.

OLD WOMAN. Welcome. (*Midwife kisses Old Woman's hand.*) May you have many who kiss your hand, my child.

Young Man kisses Midwife's hand.

MIDWIFE. Thank you, son.

YOUNG MAN. It's not labor.

MIDWIFE. Hopefully not.

WOMAN. Would you like something to drink?

MIDWIFE. Time is of essence in situations like this. Let's not delay. If there's nothing to be scared of, then I'll have coffee with you before I leave.

WOMAN. Hopefully.

MIDWIFE. Hopefully. Where's the young woman?

Woman leads Midwife to Young Woman.

MAN (*to Guard 1*). Please sit down.

Guard 1 sits. Midwife approaches Young Woman, strokes her hair.

MIDWIFE (*to Woman*). You, out!

Woman leaves the room and joins the others.

MIDWIFE. This will pass, my girl.

YOUNG WOMAN (*voice quivering*). Thank you, ma'am.

MIDWIFE. Let's talk for a minute.

YOUNG WOMAN. OK.

MIDWIFE. But you will answer my questions truthfully. OK?

YOUNG WOMAN. OK.

MIDWIFE. When did you have your first night together?

YOUNG WOMAN. Middle of December.

MIDWIFE. Did anything happen between the two of you before then? I mean like kissing or anything. Maybe you were foolish once and went a little too far. If so, you must not hide it from me.

YOUNG WOMAN. But I'm not hiding anything!

MIDWIFE. I'm asking for your own good.

YOUNG WOMAN. I swear I'm not hiding anything. (*Midwife counts on her fingers. Then she counts again.*) I'm really scared, ma'am.

MIDWIFE. There's nothing to be scared of, my child. You didn't make a mistake. According to my calculations there's at least a month before the birth.

YOUNG WOMAN. Hopefully.

MIDWIFE. If you were going into labor now, your coupling would have to have been much earlier. (*She calculates again.*) Yes, that's right. But you know, eventually, the truth always comes out. If you're not hiding anything from me, what you're feeling isn't labor. (*She looks into Young Woman's face suspiciously.*)

YOUNG WOMAN (*sees the suspicion.*) I'm not hiding anything. I swear I'm telling the truth. And how could we have been together? Our families didn't let us see each other, not even from a distance.

MIDWIFE. Can gunpowder and fire coexist, girl? Especially considering that tragic incident.

YOUNG WOMAN. Did you take care of her, too?

MIDWIFE. No, no. Am I that old? It happened a long time ago. During my grandmother's youth. But nothing like that ever happened again. Hopefully, it never will.

YOUNG WOMAN. Hopefully.

MIDWIFE. I hope you're not scared anymore.

YOUNG WOMAN (*still scared*). No.

MIDWIFE. Don't be. Fear won't help anything. Let's see, in order to be sure. Lie down where you are. Come on, lie down. (*Young Woman lies on her side.*) On your back.

Young Woman lies on her back with her head toward the audience.

YOUNG WOMAN. Like this?

MIDWIFE. Yes. Pull your legs up to your stomach. Both of them. Pull up your dress too. That's it. (*Throws Young Woman's dress a little further up.*) Raise your butt. Raise it, raise it. (*Pulls down Young Woman's underwear.*) Good girl. There's nothing to be afraid of. (*Bends over, inspects with her hand, gropes Young Woman's belly, inspects again and again, gets up.*) Get dressed.

Young Woman pulls up her underwear, gets up and waits with her hands clasped in front of her.

MIDWIFE. When did the pain start?

YOUNG WOMAN (*clearly lying*). Just before we called you.

MIDWIFE (*angry*). Don't you lie to me! When did it start? I need to know. Lie to the others if you must, but I need to know! I hope you weren't lying a minute ago!

YOUNG WOMAN. I wasn't.

MIDWIFE. I asked the first pain.

YOUNG WOMAN. Before sunrise.

MIDWIFE. Then?

YOUNG WOMAN. It was gone a little bit, then it came back.

MIDWIFE. Then?

YOUNG WOMAN. It happened again.

MIDWIFE. Then?

YOUNG WOMAN. It hasn't happened again.

MIDWIFE (*silent for a moment*). You know, girl, I know your mother well. We were neighbors for years. Surely, I'm very sorry, but I have to report this to the administrators. This is required by the rules and is for the good of society. (*Lowers her voice even more*) Tell them about your latest pain. Understood?

YOUNG WOMAN. I understand.

MIDWIFE. Or the people in the house will be in trouble, too! Don't forget this: you can't give up on God! And—maybe what you are feeling isn't labor.

YOUNG WOMAN (*desperate*). Hopefully! Will my mom and dad come too?

MIDWIFE. No! It's against the rules, that's why.

YOUNG WOMAN. Can they at least tell my mom?

MIDWIFE. It is against tradition to do such things. The trial is conducted in the house where you are. They don't ever allow emotion in matters like this. (*Quietly joins the others.*)

MAN. What happened?

MIDWIFE. Let me wash my hands.

Woman mixes boiling water with cold water and pours it over Midwife's hands.

WOMAN. Is it?

MIDWIFE (*as she dries her hands*). I won't be able to have coffee. I really wanted to but it's not meant to be. Don't be angry with me. This is the rule. I need to report this. What can I say? Let this all pass. (*To Guard 1*) You wait here! (*Leaves slowly.*)

Woman closes the door behind Midwife. Everyone is sad. Old Man is sleeping. Young Man joins Young Woman. They hug.

OLD MAN (*wakes up, looks around. He continues talking from where he left off.*) But if you ask me, it was something else. My brother didn't die naturally. They killed him! They ruthlessly got rid of him. (*He suddenly sees Guard 1.*) You guards! You! (*He jabs his hand threateningly at Guard 1.*) You killed him! You! You strangled him, and with your bare hands, too! Murderers! Murderer guards!

Woman silently tries to quiet her husband.

Blackout.

ACT III

Everyone still waits, tense. Guard 1 is trying to understand why Old Man treated him that way. Old Man has been silenced but continues to shoot angry looks at Guard 1 every once in a while. Man is pacing up and down, occasionally looking out the window.

MAN. They're coming!

WOMAN (*to Old Woman*) Well, since you can walk, you get up too. That way we'll be as respectful as possible.

MAN. Leave my mom alone!

OLD MAN. They strangled him! Murderers! Murdering guards!

OLD WOMAN. These aren't the same guards. You're confused.

OLD MAN. I'm not. He was one of them! I know it was you, you were the traitor! Traitor guard! Murderer guard!

GUARD 1 (*to Old Man*) Sir, whom did we strangle? I didn't strangle anyone! (*To the others*) What is he talking about?

MAN (*quietly to Guard 1*). My father is very old. He's old enough to believe something from years ago happened just now. Don't listen to him!

OLD MAN (*sing-song*). Murderer guard! Murderer guard!

GUARD 1. Dammit!

OLD MAN. Murderer guard! Murderer guard!

GUARD 1. This can't go on!

MAN (*He looks at Guard 1 with a look that seems to say "I'll handle this." Then he turns to Old Man*). Shut up now, Dad! Shut up! (*To the others*) They have arrived.

Old Man sulks but stays quiet. Everyone, including Old Woman, goes to the door. Man opens the door.

MAN. Come in.

WOMAN. Welcome.

OLD WOMAN. It's a pleasure to have you.

The Members of the Council of Judges come in: first President of the Council, then Female Member and Male Member. They're followed by Midwife and Guard 2.

PRESIDENT. Hello!

EVERYONE ELSE (*very respectfully*). Hello!

OLD MAN. (*He points out Guard 2 to his wife, and in a voice that can't be heard by the others*) Here, this is the other one!

Old Woman signals to Old Man that Man will get angry.

WOMAN. Where would you like to sit?

PRESIDENT (*looks around*). Let's sit somewhere sort of high. As this is how these things should be.

MAN (*pointing*). Would there be acceptable?

President looks at the other members. The members nod approvingly.

PRESIDENT. It's acceptable.

President and the members sit.

Guard 1 and Guard 2 are standing by the door. Old Man is carefully watching the members of the Council of Judges and Guards.

PRESIDENT. Bring the coffee table!

Man and Woman pick up the coffee table and place it in front of President.

MAN. Is there anything else you would like?

PRESIDENT. Our mouths may get dry as we talk. Bring us a little water! And enough cups for everyone. (*Woman puts a pitcher of water and a few wooden cups on the coffee table.*) Thank you. Where is your daughter-in-law?

WOMAN. Should she come?

PRESIDENT. Right away! Let's not waste any time.

WOMAN (*to Young Man*). I'll get her. (*Goes into Young Woman's room, beckons Young Woman.*)

PRESIDENT. We can't begin without her! (*To Old Woman*) Right?

OLD WOMAN. Right!

PRESIDENT. Everyone can have a seat. If we ask you a question, you will stand and answer. Understood?

EVERYONE ELSE. Understood.

PRESIDENT (*to the other members*). Shall we begin?

The others nod.

OLD MAN (*quietly to Old Woman*). Finally they will put the guards on trial!

IMAGE 2.5 **Arrival of the Judges.**
T. Tolga Tecer as President.
Avalanche, Akün Stage, Ankara State Theater, Ankara, 2007.
Photograph by Muzaffer Aykanat (Courtesy: Ankara State Theater).

Old Woman tries to gesture at him to shut up. Like an expert mime, she quietly tells him that Young Woman will be tried because she will give birth before the day.

OLD MAN. And now a pregnant woman! Murderers!

OLD WOMAN. Shut up!

PRESIDENT. Before we came here, we stopped by the trough. As you know, when the trough fills completely with water from melted snow, the danger is gone. However, sadly we saw that there's two fingers worth of space yet to fill. (*He demonstrates with his hand.*) That means, later today, or tomorrow at the latest, the trough will be full and the danger will be over. That is when those who left at the start of winter will come with their kids, flour, sugar, salt, vegetables, meat, and all kinds of food. And for almost three months, until the first snow falls, they will be with us. We'll have weddings, births, celebrations, festivals. When the first snow falls, the wives who have given birth and the others will leave. Until the next summer, they will work and save so that the ones staying behind can survive the next winter in comfort. Then they will come again. They will go again. But then, a little while ago, the midwife came to us and told us of an unexpected situation.

Male Member seems about to cough. Everyone is nervous. Out of habit, Female Member hands a pillow to Male Member. Male Member presses the pillow to his face and coughs quietly. He also clears his throat. He hands the pillow back to Female Member.

PRESIDENT. I'm sorry to declare that we're dealing with something that hasn't happened in fifty years. Premature birth. Like the other members I'm troubled by this. But there's nothing that can be done. We'll follow with the rules! Because this is a matter of the people's safety, of life and death!

Male Member again seems about to cough. One pillow won't be enough this time, so the others cover his face with several. A little later he grows still. He has died. They carry Male Member to an elevated area. Everyone pays their respects.

PRESIDENT. Now let's do what we have to before losing more time. Let's get down to business. (*To Midwife*) When were you informed?

MIDWIFE (*getting up*). A little while ago.

PRESIDENT. Your conclusion?

MIDWIFE. I came right away and checked her. I then let you know of the situation. It pains me to say this, but she will give birth very soon.

PRESIDENT. Are you sure?

MIDWIFE. Absolutely.

PRESIDENT. You should double-check.

MIDWIFE. There's no need. All signs indicate that the baby is coming.

PRESIDENT. You may sit. You two! (*Young Woman and Young Man get up.*) We have determined that, normally, you wouldn't go into labor for another month. Nevertheless, you're about to go into labor before the danger has passed. You know that this is the greatest crime, that it puts others' lives in danger, right?

YOUNG MAN. We do.

YOUNG WOMAN. We do.

YOUNG MAN. But this isn't our fault!

PRESIDENT. What do you mean?

YOUNG MAN. Our elders made the calculation. They decided what day we could be together. That was our first night. Until that night, I was allowed to see my wife only from a distance. We could never even be side by side.

MAN. Mr. President, if you will allow me, I would like to say something.

PRESIDENT. Keep it short.

MAN. My son is telling the truth. We kept them apart until the day.

WOMAN. We didn't even let them hold hands.

PRESIDENT. Do not speak without asking for permission. Understood?

WOMAN. Understood, Mr. President.

PRESIDENT. Let's assume everything happened as you say. I'm having a hard time understanding where you're going with this.

YOUNG MAN. This will be a premature birth.

MIDWIFE (*gets up*). Yes, Mr. President. This will be a premature birth.

YOUNG MAN. That means we're guilty of nothing.

Silence.

PRESIDENT. Either way, what difference does it make? We're not discussing whether or not this is a premature birth. We look only at the result. Right now, before the danger has passed, the Young Woman is about to go into labor. That's all we care about. However, if there were marital relations too soon, in violation of the rules, that would interest us as well. But it wouldn't change the results. What we must do now is clear. (*Tacitly, he seeks the approval of the others.*) This young woman will be put into a coffin without delay, and then she will be buried in the ground. It will be of consolation to us for you to know that we're sad about this decision.

YOUNG MAN. Mr. President!

PRESIDENT. There's nothing left to discuss. Because this Young Woman may go into labor any second now. Need I remind you of what that could cause? Listen, if the midwife has an objection to this, the execution will of course be stayed, and the situation can be discussed. (*To Midwife*) That's because in this situation you are the only person who has the right to object. Do you have anything to say against this decision?

MIDWIFE. No, Mr. President.

PRESIDENT. Let the rules be applied before more time is wasted!

OLD MAN. They're not trying the guards!

Man and Old Woman signal Old Man to hush.

YOUNG MAN. My wife is being punished for something that isn't our fault. Why, because the rules say so? We have done nothing that was not within the rules. Our wedding, our first night, all happened at the prescribed time.

PRESIDENT (*angry*). We've been through this, son. Beside, this is the first time I've ever heard of anything like this. I don't know if it would do you any good to be reminded of why the children of this land immediately get jobs wherever they go. Because they don't object to anything! Let's not forget that the word for "unrest" has been struck off our dictionary because the rules have been administered without fail! (*He grows even more angry.*) What do you mean? Should we discuss the rules and let so many people die?

YOUNG MAN (*very emotional*). Don't let anyone die! But don't let my wife die either!

PRESIDENT. I understand your pain, young man. We were young once, too, We have also been in love. But one has to know how to sacrifice so that other people can live.

YOUNG MAN (*about to cry*). Birth doesn't happen all of a sudden! Please delay a little longer.

PRESIDENT. Not possible. I can't endanger the whole village. It's either your wife or everyone. All of us. There's no middle ground! If there was a solution that would allow us all to live, do you think I wouldn't implement that? (*He is resolute.*) The execution will happen as soon as possible. The rules will be administered! What could we do if your wife goes into labor now? A single scream let out during birth is enough. What are we going to do about the cries of the newborn baby? Wouldn't the mountains come down on our heads? (*He suddenly becomes stern.*) If you go on talking we may have to take the same decision for you too! Be quiet now!

YOUNG MAN. Mr. President!

PRESIDENT. I'm warning you! Don't forget! If speech is silver, silence is golden! This has been our principle for centuries. (*He signals Guards to take action.*)

IMAGE 2.6 **The ones resisting the trial are being silenced.**
T. Tolga Tecer as President, Nurtekin Odabaşı as Old Man, Rengin Samurçay as Old Woman, and others.
Avalanche, Akün Stage, Ankara State Theater, Ankara, 2007.
Photograph by Muzaffer Aykanat (*Courtesy: Ankara State Theater*).

OLD MAN. They're not trying the guards! They will bury not the murderers but the innocent!

PRESIDENT. What the hell is he talking about?

OLD MAN. For God's sake, man, you should be prosecuting the people who strangled my brother!

PRESIDENT. What are you saying?

OLD MAN. Prosecute the murderers! If you have the guts, prosecute them! But you can't! Because they'd strangle you immediately!

PRESIDENT. Gag him, too! (*Guard 1 tries to gag Old Man with a rag.*) Hurry up!

OLD MAN (*tries to fight them off*). Now I understand my brother even better. I understand him very well!

PRESIDENT (*to Guard 2*). Prepare the other one too!

GUARD 2. Yes, sir! (*Moves to gag Young Woman.*)

PRESIDENT. You've surprised me, young man. However, I'll blame this on your grief and forgive you.

GUARD 2 (*has gagged Young Woman and tied her hands behind her back*). Done, sir.

PRESIDENT (*signals for him to blindfold her as well*). Finish the job! (*Guard 2 blindfolds her. Young Woman trembles in fear.*) All right. (*To the others*) Nobody leaves! Until this business is finished, you will all stay in your houses. (*To Guard 1*) You stay here. (*To Female Member*) Come on, get up. We will witness the administration of the rules.

President and Female Member stand. Guard 2 has a hard time taking Young Woman who is resisting, moaning in protest. At a warning from President, Guard 2 brings Young Woman toward the door, almost dragging her. Behind them slowly walk President and Female Member. While the others wait quietly, Young Man has opened the box of ammunition and loaded a bullet into one of the rifles.

YOUNG MAN (*He points the rifle into the air*). Stop now!

For a moment everyone stops. This is a complete surprise.

PRESIDENT. What do you intend to do, my child?

YOUNG MAN. I said stop!

FEMALE MEMBER. What is the meaning of this? What is he doing?

YOUNG MAN. Don't make me pull the trigger!

PRESIDENT. How did this happen?

FEMALE MEMBER. Won't the rifle fire if you pull the trigger? When the rifle fires . . . Oh my God!

PRESIDENT. But, we'll all die!

YOUNG MAN. Yes. We'll die! Either my wife lives or we'll all die together!

Silence.

MAN. Put the gun down.

WOMAN. Do you want to kill us as well?

MAN. Won't we all die together?

YOUNG MAN. Dad, stay out of this.

MAN. How can I stay out of it? Come to your senses, son.

YOUNG MAN. Should my wife die? I have to do whatever I can so that my wife and my unborn child can live!

MAN. What can you do?

OLD WOMAN. We'll all die together!

WOMAN. You're still young. There will be other women. It's in your hands. You can have a child with some other woman.

OLD WOMAN. You will be murdering your parents!

OLD MAN. I'm proud of my grandson!

YOUNG MAN. You don't understand me! (*To President*) Nobody move! Go back to your seats. I said go!

President and Female Member return to their seats. Guard 2 brings Young Woman back to her seat. At Young Man's signal, Guard 2 removes her gag, blindfold, and bonds. Silence.

IMAGE 2.7 **Young Woman on trial.**
Leyla Aykan Gülener as Young Woman.
Avalanche, Akün Stage, Ankara State Theater, Ankara, 2007.
Photograph by Muzaffer Aykanat (Courtesy: Ankara State Theater).

PRESIDENT. My mouth is dry. Can I have some water?

YOUNG MAN. Drink!

> *President drinks some water. So does Female Member.*

PRESIDENT. What will happen now?

FEMALE MEMBER. What are we waiting for?

YOUNG MAN (*to Guard 1*). You! Dad, you too. Go and check the trough! Let's see what the situation is! Don't waste time!

> *Man and Guard 2 leave.*

IMAGE 2.8 **The trial continues.**
Leyla Aykan Gülener as Young Woman.
Avalanche, Akün Stage, Ankara State Theater, Ankara, 2007.
Photograph by Muzaffer Aykanat (Courtesy: Ankara State Theater).

OLD MAN. Let's put the guards on trial!

> *Old Woman quietens Old Man. Everyone waits. President and Female Member are in a state of fear and confusion. After a long while, Man and Guard 1 return.*

MAN. One finger!

GUARD 1. Yes, one finger.

YOUNG MAN. And her pain hasn't returned. Maybe the midwife was wrong and this isn't labor! But because of your impatience, my wife almost died. Look! You see? Do you see any pain?

PRESIDENT. What are you saying son? Is the midwife lying? You may not care about us, but your mother, your father. They will die! Don't you have any mercy for them?

Suddenly Young Woman starts writhing in pain.

PRESIDENT. Oh my God!

MIDWIFE. She's going into labor!

YOUNG MAN (*to Guard 1*). Gag her!

Guard 1 gags Young Woman.

YOUNG MAN. Take her to the other room.

As Guard 1 takes Young Woman to the other room, Old Man silently claps in delight.

YOUNG MAN (*to Midwife*). Go. Mom, you help as well.

MIDWIFE (*to Woman*) Bring a washbasin and hot water! Quick!

YOUNG MAN. Quick, Mom!

PRESIDENT (*terrified*). What about the baby's cry!

FEMALE MEMBER (*terrified*). Cries!

PRESIDENT. We'll all die!

FEMALE MEMBER. We'll die!

OLD MAN. I came here to die anyway. It doesn't matter. Now I understand my brother even better. I want to scream, too, before I die. I want to scream! Right now!

OLD WOMAN. Don't! Don't you do any such thing!

MAN. I'm your son, Dad!

WOMAN. I guess this is the end of us.

MAN. You'll get me killed too! (*Covers Old Man's mouth with his hand.*)

WOMAN (*to Young Man*). I raised you. Did I raise you so you could be the agent of my death? I won't give you my blessing!

YOUNG MAN. Shut up!

Midwife signals Guard 1 to leave. Guard 1 joins the others. Guard 2 approaches Young Man stealthily. Just as he is about to grab

Young Man's arm, he is noticed. Young Man hits Guard 2 with the stock of the rifle.

YOUNG MAN. Don't! Don't you try that again!

PRESIDENT (*to Guard 1*). You idiot!

YOUNG MAN. Got it?

GUARD 1. Got it.

In the other room, Young Woman is lying down with her head toward the audience. The birth is happening silently. Midwife is gesturing instructions to Woman.

FEMALE MEMBER (*scared*). But . . . they will have to hold the baby's mouth shut all the time because it will let out one scream after the other.

PRESIDENT. They have to hold the baby's mouth shut until the trough is full.

Young Woman's moaning has increased. The hoarse moans come from deep within her. The moans stop suddenly. Midwife lifts the baby, covering its mouth with one hand .

The baby slips out of Midwife's hands into the washbasin. An incredible scream is heard.

As these deafening laugh-like screams are heard one after the other, Midwife gets a hold of the baby again.

There is total silence.

The echoes of the screams are heard.

Silence again.

Everyone waits fearfully for the avalanche. Some also pray.

There's no sign of an avalanche.

PRESIDENT. Nothing happened!

FEMALE MEMBER. I guess there won't be an avalanche.

YOUNG MAN. Shut up!

More silence.

Despite his wife's attempts to stop him, Old Man grabs the rifle from Young Man's hands and opens the door. He lets out a colossal scream.

A little later, the echo of the scream is heard. Then he fires the rifle. Its echo is heard. The anxious waiting is replaced by displays of happiness. Drumming and pipe music accompany the sounds of rifle fire outside.

The End

(*Facing page*) IMAGE 2.9 **Old Man lets out a colossal scream.**

Nurtekin Odabaşı as Old Man.
Avalanche. Akün Stage, Ankara State Theater, Ankara, 2007.
Photograph by Muzaffer Aykanat (*Courtesy: Ankara State Theater*).

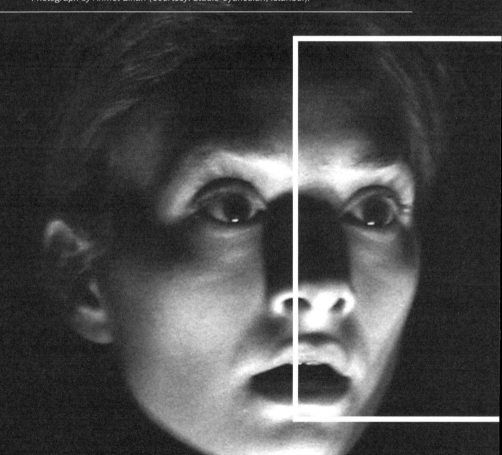

CHARACTERS

CREON

TIRESIAS

ANTIGONE

ISMENE

HAEMON

EURYDICE

CHORUS

EURYDICE'S CRY

ŞAHİKA TEKAND

NOTES ON THE PLAY

Eurydice's Cry premiered at the Suzuki Theater, Toga, Japan, in July 2007, with the following cast and crew:

Creon	Şerif Erol
Tiresias	Yiğit Özşener
Antigone	Arda Kurşunoğlu
Ismene	Ridade Tuncel
Haemon	Cem Bender
Eurydice	Şahika Tekand
Chorus	Ahmet Sarıcan, Gülşah Karahasan, Hakan Turutoğlu, Deniz Karaoğlu, Umut Kırcalı, Zeynep Papuççuoğlu, Özgür Özcan, Jaki Baruh, Atilla Çoşar, İlksen Gözde Olgun, Korhan Soydan
Director	Şahika Tekand
Assistant Directors	Özlem Özhabeş, Ayşegül Cengiz Akman, Verda Habif, Nilgün Kurtar, Ulushan Ulusman, Tulu Ülgen
Stage Designer	Esat Tekand
Light Designer	Şahika Tekand
Costume Designer	Esat Tekand
Light-Performers	Ayşegül Cengiz Akman, Nilgün Kurtar

The events in *Eurydice*'s *Cry* follow the events in *Where is Oedipus?* (2002) and *Oedipus in Exile* (2004). These three texts, inspired by Sophocles's tragedies, often quote each other. For instance, some of Oedipus's lines in the first and the second tragedies are are given, respectively, to Creon and Antigone in this one. This requires the characters to react not just emotionally but also objectively. The actors are expected to pay attention to the way their character was played in the production of the earlier texts.

The Chorus's primary function is to create an ambience. It treats language as music, although it is aware of what the speeches articulate.

The main action is expressed through a matrix which requires a repetition of a limited number of movements. Through this matrix, the Chorus's stance should evolve—from status quo to rebellion.

The actors face an additional obligation in the performance of the play. To express themselves, they only have access to a limited number of movements and some key words, and they are required to respond to the light design. These compulsory movements and strict rules should make the stage into a simulation field and give the actors' performance a genuineness similar to that of a tightrope-walker performing without a safety net.

The stage should be designed to represent Thebes's utter ruin.

The lights must be controlled manually. Those who control the lights must be challenged in the same way as the Chorus and the stage performers.

The play must start at a slow pace and gradually reach a speed requiring endurance. The temperature of the stage must increase —literally changing from blue to red. This can be achieved by gradually intensifying the rhythm of both sound and light.

EURYDICE'S CRY
Şahika Tekand

PROLOGOS
(Chorus)

CHORUS. He has been buried!
  (*Pause*)
  Haaa!
  (*Pause*)
  He has been buried!
CHORUS MEMBER. Haa!
  (*Pause*)
CHORUS. He has been buried. Polyneices has been buried!
  (*Darkness; pause*)
CHORUS MEMBER 1. Co! . . . (*Pose change*)
CHORUS MEMBER 2. Da! . . . (*Pose change*)
CHORUS. Bur! (*Pose change*)
CHORUS MEMBER 3. Da! (*Pose change*)
CHORUS. Blackest . . . (*Pose change*)
  Alas! (*Pose change*)
  Blackest earth . . . (*Pose change*)
  Covered with blackest earth . . . (*Pose change*)
CHORUS MEMBER 4. Polyneices has been buried! (*Pose change*)
CHORUS. Haaa! (*Pose change*)
  Alas! (*Pose change*)
  Covered with black earth . . . (*Pose change*)
  Who buried Polyneices? (*Pose change*)
  Pause.
CHORUS MEMBER 5. Against the law! (*Pose change*)
CHORUS MEMBER. Against the law! (*Pose change*)
CHORUS. How could the law be violated? (*Pose change*)

Haaa! (*Pose change*)
The law was violated! (*Pose change*)
The law was violated! (*Pose change*)
Who! . . . Who! . . . Who did this! . . . (*Pose change*)
Who dares violate the law? (*Pose change*)
Who would be so arrogant and go against the king?
(*Pose change*)
Who! Who! (*Pose change*)
There isn't a single trace! (*Pose change*)
Dry earth, hard as rock. (*Pose change*)
Neither wheel nor foot. (*Pose change*)
Haaa! (*Pose change*)
Gods! (*Pose change*)
Apollo, son of Zeus, (*Pose change*)
Phoebus, who shoots his arrows far, (*Pose change*)
Immortal Athena, (*Pose change*)
Bacchus with a wreath on his head, (*Pose change*)
Help! (*Pose change*)

EPISODE I
(Chorus, Creon)

CREON. Who?

CHORUS. Ha! Creon!

CREON. Who is this?

Chorus poses silently.

CREON. Who is this raving rebel who dares to revolt against the state?

Chorus poses silently.

CREON. Who is this who attempts this mad crime? Who is this defiant person, disobeying my order?

CHORUS. Creon! Ruler of our city!

There isn't a single trace of the criminal!

There isn't a single trace!
Dry earth, hard as rock!
Neither wheel nor foot!
There isn't a single trace of the one who buried the corpse!

CREON. Such arrogance! How can one dare threaten the law and order of Thebes after all the suffering the city has endured?

CHORUS. How! How!
Who dares break the law?
Who arrogantly challenges the king?
Who!

CREON. My fellow Thebans!

CHORUS. Creon! Son of Menoeceus!

CREON. I know very well that you are the most staunch pillars of this state. We've shared the same cursed fate all this time. But today, your allegiance to this state will be tested once again.

Chorus poses silently.

CREON. I know Thebes has suffered undeservedly. Now is the time for peace and order. How can we allow a rebel to destroy that?

CHORUS. Dry earth, hard as rock!
Neither wheel nor foot!
There isn't a single trace!

CREON. Thebans, for years I've seen you hold sacred this state and this throne and seen your loyalty to Oedipus.

CHORUS. Labdacus's descendants . . .

CREON. I've noticed how you stayed loyal to his memory even though, on foreign soil, he cursed his own sons and Thebes itself with his dying breath.

CHORUS. Labdacus's descendants have been afflicted with catastrophe . . .

CREON. And the gods know very well that I, also, have honored and always respected the state and the throne of Laius. After my poor sister, Jocasta, killed herself and Oedipus left the city in shame, I still loved his children, cherished them like my own.

CHORUS. Labdacus's descendants have been afflicted with
catastrophe through the generations.

CREON. I always respected his sons, who I raised as my own.

CHORUS. Labdacus's descendants have been afflicted with
catastrophe through the generations.
May the ever-present curse finally leave.

CREON. But Polyneices's never-ending rage, like his father's, brought
trouble to this city.

CHORUS. The curse! The curse!
Labdacus's descendants have been afflicted with
catastrophe through the generations.
May the ever-present curse finally leave.

CREON. Eteocles and Polyneices, two brothers, sharing both blood
and destiny. At the end of a dire war which was caused by
Polyneices's ambition and enmity, bringing Thebes to the
brink of catastrophe yet again . . .

CHORUS. Huh!

CREON. . . . I lost my firstborn son, Megareus, and they took each
other's lives . . .

CHORUS. Unfortunate sons of unfortunate Oedipus
The curse of their father, who was expelled and humiliated
by his own children, shook and demolished them.
His eyes, cloaked in darkness, waited for the moment of
revenge.
Children, borne of a sinful marriage, suffered their whole
lives.

CREON. I, Creon, as their uncle and closest living relative, have
taken over the affairs of state. I am ready to shoulder the
responsibility for Thebes. Therefore, I commanded Eteocles
be buried with full ceremonies, for he died in the war,
fighting heroically for his homeland. As for Polyneices, I
commanded that his body be left exposed to the vultures and
dogs, deprived of ceremonies or even a grave . . .

Chorus is silent and still.

CREON. Because he wanted to make you slaves and extinguish the flames of his wrath with the blood of his relatives.

Chorus is silent and still.

CREON. Because any statesman who holds his tongue in fear, in the face of a rebellion, is a traitor in my eyes.

CHORUS. The curse! The curse!
> Labdacus's descendants have been afflicted with catastrophe
> > through the generations.
> May the ever-present curse finally leave.

CREON. Only strict laws that distinguish between villain and innocent and between loyalty and treason can protect the civil order.

CHORUS. If only the gods would help us . . .
> So all words and deeds may
> Reach the sacredness
> of divine law.

CREON. One can find legitimate reasons to pardon the criminals, and reasons to forgive them.

CHORUS. The laws that were born on Olympus:
> That do not sleep or forget,
> That do not deteriorate or age
> And live on.

CREON. After repenting and serving their sentences, criminals may be allowed to live among us again.

CHORUS. The traitor, the son of arrogance and pride;
> The more he is nourished and grows,
> The more he sees himself in high places.

CREON. But traitors cannot be shown mercy under any circumstances. One can't be silent when law and order are at stake.

CHORUS. If only the gods would help us . . .
> So all words and deeds may
> Reach the sacredness
> Of divine law.
> The laws that were born on Olympus:

That do not sleep or forget,
That do not deteriorate or age
And live on.
The traitor, the son of arrogance and pride;
The more he is nourished and grows,
The more he sees himself in high places.
What can be done?
How?
How can we find him?
Who!
Who!
Who dares to violate the law?
Who arrogantly challenges the king?
Who!

CREON. I ask you now . . .

CHORUS. Haa!

CREON. The body of a traitor was buried in spite of my specific order. Were there no witnesses? Speak up!

CHORUS. There isn't a single trace!

CREON. The law orders the rebel to be punished immediately. Even a shadow sighted or a voice overheard—a small trace can be of great help. Tell me!

CHORUS. There isn't a single trace of the criminal!

CREON. How can such a crime be committed so easily if there are no accomplices, no one who turned a blind eye? Tell me!

CHORUS. Haa!

CREON. Speak up!

CHORUS. Alas!
Dry earth, hard as rock!
Neither wheel nor foot!
There isn't a single trace!
There isn't a single trace of the criminal.

CREON. Wasn't anyone guarding the corpse?

Chorus poses silently.

CREON. Has not even one person seen anything?

Chorus poses silently.

CREON. Is that possible?

Chorus poses silently.

CREON. What mortal could disappear so skillfully, without a trace, if they had no help or support ?

Chorus poses silently.

CREON. It seems clear that the traitor, his accomplices, and witnesses are here, among us.

CHORUS. What can be done?
How!
How can we be exonerated?

CREON. Will you eject them from your midst, or will you surrender to a defeatist idea?

CHORUS. Haa!

CREON. Speak up! The day has come to show your allegiance to the state! Make your decision! Don't keep silent and drown yourselves in the mire of this crime!

CHORUS. Alas!
If I knew, wouldn't I tell?
What mortal would value the life of another
Higher than his own precious life?
One who is implicated
Will die of fear before his death.
The Heavens and the Earth are filled with flames of accusation.
The soil is nourished only by blackest fear.
If I knew, wouldn't I tell?

CREON. Either talk or bear the consequences. Nothing will deter me in this case. With the help of Zeus I will catch the criminal. Now, I tell you all . . .

Chorus poses silently.

CREON. Whoever did this will be arrested and brought to me immediately. Or else . . .

CHORUS. Haa!

CREON. Or else I shall assume whoever stays silent is a traitor! I will not permit cowardly silence to destroy this city.

CHORUS. Alas!
>The Heavens and the Earth are filled with flames of accusation
>The soil is nourished only by blackest fear.
>(*Pause*)
>What can be done?
>How!

IMAGE 3.2 **Chorus members unified in an aggressive pose that signifies their allegiance to Creon.**
Deniz Karaoğlu, Umut Kırcalı, İlksen Gözde Olgun as Chorus members. *Eurydice's Cry*, Suzuki Theater, Toga, Japan, 2006.
Photograph by Ahmet Elhan (Courtesy: Studio Oyuncuları, Istanbul).

How can we be exonerated?
Gods!

CREON. Now only the dead will be allowed to stay silent in this city!

CHORUS. Haaa!
If I knew, wouldn't I tell?
What mortal would value the life of another higher than his
    own precious life?
One who is implicated
Will die of fear before his death.
Apollo, son of Zeus,

IMAGE 3.3 **Chorus members unified in another pose signifying their allegiance to Creon.**
Deniz Karaoğlu, Umut Kırcalı, Özlem Özhabeş as Chorus members.
Eurydice's Cry, Suzuki Theater, Toga, Japan, 2006.
Photograph by Ahmet Elhan (Courtesy: Studio Oyuncuları, Istanbul).

Phoebus, who shoots his arrows far,
Immortal Athena,
Bacchus with a wreath on his head.

CREON. You are pleading . . .

CHORUS. Help us!

CREON. You are asking for help . . .

CHORUS. Gods!

CREON. Help to soothe your fear . . .

CHORUS. Gods, help!

CREON. If you don't give me a clue, I will lose my patience.

CHORUS. Help! I call you all, one by one.

CREON. If one of you saw who buried the traitor Polyneices . . .

CHORUS. Who!

CREON. If someone knows the instigator of this dark rebellion, this treacherous revolt . . .

CHORUS. Who!

CREON. You must not stay silent. Everyone in this country, this man . . .

CHORUS. Who!

CREON. . . . whoever he may be, I forbid you to protect him. This villainous, corrupted creature . . .

CHORUS. Who!

CREON. . . . I command that all homes be closed to him. Whoever pities the traitor shall need pity himself, may the gods be my witness.

CHORUS. What can be done? How! How can we be exonerated? Gods!

CREON. Think well, Thebes, keep evil away from your home, and don't darken your destiny by remaining silent.

CHORUS. Ha! (*Short sharp pose.*)

CREON. If the order of this city collapses, it will do so upon you all, and no one will stay sound.

CHORUS. Alas!
    If I knew, wouldn't I tell?
    If I knew, wouldn't I tell?
    Gods help us!
    Apollo, son of Zeus,
    Phoebus, who shoots his arrows far,
    Immortal Athena,
    Bacchus with a wreath on his head.
    Help!

CREON (*loudly, with certainty*). Quiet. Be quiet before I lose my
    temper!

CHORUS. Gods!

CREON. Do the gods care about the carcass of a traitor?

CHORUS. Gods! Help!

CREON. Do the gods help those who shelter a traitor among
    themselves?

CHORUS. Help! I call you all, one by one.

CREON. How arrogant is he who flouts my power and decrees?

CHORUS. The Heavens and the Earth are filled with flames of
    accusation

CREON. What was this insolent one thinking when he did this?

CHORUS. The soil is nourished only by blackest fear.

CREON. Will the gods accept a traitor—who has been fighting
    against his kin, who has come to destroy this ancient city,
    Thebes—into their soil?

CHORUS. The Heavens and the Earth are filled with flames of
        accusation
    The soil is noured only by blackest fear.

CREON. With Zeus as my witness, this villainous, insidious creature,
    who, for now, wanders among you . . .

CHORUS. Who!

CREON. . . . will be caught at all costs . . .

CHORUS. Who!

CREON. . . . and be put, alive, into a tomb and stoned to death.

CHORUS. Haa!

CREON. Damn all instigators. Damn those who harbor them. Damn the ones who know, yet remain silent! And let me say this: if, I, Creon, even without knowing—

CHORUS (*quickly*). Not knowing . . .

CREON. . . . had this man—who threatened the power of this state—

CHORUS (*quickly*). Not knowing . . . not knowing . . .
Not knowing the shape of his fate.

CREON. . . . living in my house, in my confidence, may the curse, the curse I cast on others be visited on me!

Blackout.

FIRST STASIMON
(Chorus, Antigone)

ANTIGONE. They will kill . . .

Darkness; a pause.

CHORUS. Haa!
(*Darkness; a shorter pause*)
They will kill . . .
(*Pause*)
By stoning
By stoning to death
(*Darkness; a pause*)
Against the law!
Against the law!
How could the law be violated?
(*Louder*) How could the law be violated?
(*Darkness; a pause*)
If only the gods would help us

So all words and deeds may
Reach the sacredness
Of divine law.
The laws that were born on Olympus:
That do not sleep or forget,
That do not deteriorate or age
And live on.
The traitor, the son of arrogance and pride;
The more he is nourished and grows,
The more he sees himself in high places.
Not knowing the shape of his fate.

Blackout.

EPISODE II
(Tiresias, Creon, Chorus, Antigone)

TIRESIAS. Pity, what a pity!

CHORUS and CREON. Tiresias!

TIRESIAS. Your words will bring you misfortune.

CREON. Tiresias, you are one who intuits all that is known and unknown. Even if you're blind, you know what catastrophe has befallen the city. A maniac in Thebes has defied my commands. He has threatened law and order. But there is neither evidence nor the smallest trace. Help us!

CHORUS. There is no trace of the criminal! Help us!

CREON. Cleanse the taint this crime has put on the state.

CHORUS. There isn't a single trace!
Dry earth, hard as rock!
Neither wheel nor foot!
There isn't a single trace of the criminal!

TIRESIAS. It's dreadful to have knowledge if it does not help the one who knows!

CHORUS. For the love of the gods . . .

CREON. Don't turn your back on us! Tell us what you know!

TIRESIAS. Creon, we both walk the same path . . .

CREON. You know I value your insights. Only your prophecies can help us.

CHORUS. Tell us what you know!

TIRESIAS. . . . but only one of us sees it.

CHORUS. The Heavens and the Earth are filled with flames of accusation.
The soil is nourished only by blackest fear.
We're begging!
We're begging!
Tell us what you know!

CREON. Be frank, Tiresias. Tell us what you know.

TIRESIAS. The person who is striving to know has to pay the price of knowledge.

CHORUS. For the love of the gods, don't turn your back on us.
Tell us what you know!

CREON. What further price must I pay? I was a father to the children of Oedipus, who, with his sins, brought shame to his line. I have not let them down. But Polyneices, whom I treated like my son, drew a sword against me and my city. To that sword I lost my son, Megareus. What further price must I pay, Tiresias? If you are not going to help, then why are you here?

CHORUS. Why?

TIRESIAS. The truth is on the razor's edge.

CREON. What can be worse than what's already happening? What kind of truth is this that you don't want to speak?

CHORUS. For the love of the gods, tell us what you know!

TIRESIAS. Only when the seeker is ready does the truth become evident.

CREON. Don't you see how I strive to reveal the truth? Don't you hear the people's anguish?

CHORUS. We're begging!

CREON. Don't you hear their pleas?

TIRESIAS. In vain!

CHORUS. We're begging!

CREON. Do not make this city beg more, Tiresias!

TIRESIAS. In vain!

CHORUS. We're begging you!

TIRESIAS. Catastrophe is inevitable.

Chorus poses silently.

CREON. These people who beg you have sacrificed their husbands and their sons for the salvation of this city. They deserve to know the truth. Why won't you tell them?

CHORUS. Speak up!

TIRESIAS. Not piety, not prayer, not even sacrifices are accepted.

CHORUS. Haaa!

TIRESIAS. No bird flies over our heads, bringing us auspicious news.

CHORUS. Alas!

TIRESIAS. This city is tainted with such malice. Neither Ishtaros nor Phasis could eliminate it.

CHORUS. Gods!
Those words strike me like a bolt of lightning
A storm of fear smothers my soul
Calamitous clouds pile up

CREON. There is nothing I haven't done for the salvation of this city. However, this instigation will not cease until its roots are severed.

TIRESIAS. Everything is dissolving. All that is sacred is being trod upon.

CHORUS. Those words strike me like a bolt of lightning
A storm of fear smothers my soul
Calamitous clouds pile up
(*Pause*)

Who!

Who!

Who could be so insolent, without fear of trouble?

Who!

TIRESIAS. If at least one person could have seen . . .

CREON. Tiresias! Speak up: What could he have seen?

CHORUS. Speak up!

TIRESIAS. If at least one person could have thought?

CREON. What should he have thought?

CHORUS. Speak up!

TIRESIAS. Think!

CHORUS. Speak up!

CREON. Since the moment you arrived you've been hiding behind allusions, hiding the truth. Why?

CHORUS. Why?

TIRESIAS. Think!

CREON. Why won't you speak?

CHORUS. Why?

CREON. You've exhausted my patience. From now on I will not hold back what goes through my mind.

CHORUS. Creon!

CREON. Your silence makes you an accomplice.

CHORUS. Don't!

CREON. It's as if you're allied not with Thebes but the traitors who came to destroy this city.

CHORUS. Don't!

CREON. You are an accomplice!

CHORUS. Don't!

CREON. It is well known that prophecies of catastrophe are most valuable. That's why all oracles are fond of chaos.

CHORUS. Don't!

TIRESIAS. And those in power are addicted to sycophants.

CHORUS. Tiresias!

CREON. How dare you?

CHORUS. The more he is nourished and grows,
    The more he sees himself in high places.

TIRESIAS. How heroic it is to kill those who are already dead . . .

CHORUS. Tiresias!

TIRESIAS. How fair it is to stab corpses . . .

CHORUS. Don't!

CREON. Where do you get the nerve to talk to me like this? How
    dare you? I am the king of this city.

TIRESIAS. And that is your disease!

CHORUS. Tiresias! Don't!

CREON (*furious, mocking*). Hah! When I'm subjected to such insult,
    the blind oracle, Tiresias, doesn't stop from joining in, is that
    so?

CHORUS. If a mortal oracle makes a prediction,
    I would not believe before
    Seeing the words proved right beyond doubt.
    I cannot agree, surely, before
    Seeing the words proved right beyond doubt.

TIRESIAS. Give unto Hades what is Hades's!
    Refrain from stabbing corpses.
    Give the dead what they deserve.

CHORUS. Alas!

CREON. Do you think your vile words will go unpunished? Who
    taught you truth, your art of prophecy?

CHORUS. Don't!

CREON. Talk however you wish! They bring no harm to me! But you
    cannot say these words again and go unpunished!

TIRESIAS. The power of truth!

CHORUS. The power of truth!

CREON. The power of truth, yes. But not for you . . .

CHORUS. Don't!

CREON. Not for a man whose soul and ears are as closed as his eyes.

CHORUS. Don't!

TIRESIAS. You trust the power in your hands too much!

CREON. Are these your own ideas or are they your accomplice's?

TIRESIAS. I'm not a slave. I will be nobody's subject.

CHORUS. How can truth be determined?
> How can the truthfulness of words be determined?
> Dark suspicion is settling in my heart,
> A mad fear raging in my chest
> Like the rising sound
> Of drums
> (*Pause*)
> How can the truthfulness of words be determined?

CREON. It's a good thing to attain supremacy . . .

CHORUS. Stop!

CREON. . . . holding the power . . .

CHORUS. Stop!

CREON. Being mighty and powerful!

CHORUS. Stop! Don't!

CREON. Though it generates such jealousy!

TIRESIAS. Be careful, Creon. You're crossing the line!

CREON. How come? How come a blind oracle dares reproach me, a king?

CHORUS. . . . sees himself in high places.

TIRESIAS. What use are your eyes if you don't see the calamity upon you and the fate to which you are leading the city?

CHORUS. The son of arrogance and pride,
> The more he is nourished and grows,
> The more he sees himself in high places.

CREON. If you were so worried about this city, the fate of this city, where were you when the enemy took the seven gates of Thebes?

CHORUS. Where?

CREON. What did you do to save Thebes and its citizens when it was burning in the fires of war?

CHORUS. Speak up!

CREON. Not everyone could do that of course. That required courage . . .

CHORUS. If an oracle . . .

If an oracle would stand up.

CREON. But I, Creon, as soon as I was came to power, brought an end to the chaos, without appealing to birds and the gods. I made laws and instituted peace and order to the land. That is the truth, and you aid the criminal by attacking my decisions!

CHORUS. If an oracle would stand up . . .

If . . .

If . . .

(*Pause*)

If a mortal oracle makes a prediction,

I would not believe before

Seeing the words proved right beyond doubt.

I cannot agree, surely, before

Seeing the words proved right beyond doubt.

TIRESIAS. You've spoken! Now it's my turn!

CREON. You are a master of words. But I have no intention of listening to your lies.

TIRESIAS. You don't want to hear my prophecies when they are against you.

CHORUS. Listen!

TIRESIAS. You don't want to hear the truth!

CHORUS. Listen!

CREON. I know! You'll try to prove that I made unfair decisions!

CHORUS. Listen!

TIRESIAS. You are unaware of the calamity . . .

CREON. How can one bear . . .

CHORUS. Listen!

TIRESIAS. . . . That will deprive you of your loved ones . . .

CREON. How can one bear these words?

CHORUS. Listen!

CREON. No!

TIRESIAS. . . . That will put you in your place!

CREON. You are exhausting my patience. You don't know how to speak to a sovereign!

TIRESIAS. Find evil not in my words, but in yourself!

CREON. You haven't made a single accurate prophecy since you arrived. You won't reveal the criminal even though you know who it is. With your words you only try to harass me. If there's anyone who expects me to rescind my order for fear of these lies, putting my sovereignty in jeopardy, they're very wrong. Even if all the eagles of Cronion take the corpse to Zeus's throne as fodder . . .

CHORUS. Creon!

CREON. . . . even if the shredded, torn, scattered, and decayed pieces of carrion stink to the house of the gods . . .

CHORUS. Haaa!
Don't!

CREON. . . . I will not be afraid, and even then I will not allow this traitor to be interred!

CHORUS. Creon!

TIRESIAS. Creon, go no further. You are crossing the line.

CHORUS. Don't!

CREON. In vain! I made a promise to this city.

TIRESIAS. You have aggrieved this city! Very soon screams of mourning will rise from the hopeless walls of the city!

Chorus pauses.

TIRESIAS. You will not be spared the pain! You will be left all alone!

CHORUS. I'm wavering . . .

CREON. In vain!

CHORUS. I'm wavering . . .

TIRESIAS. You will go through the same suffering and will not spared the pain! You will be left all alone! You'll rule only a desert. You'll be destroyed!

CHORUS. Haaa!

Alas!

If you will rule in this land,

It's better to rule over people than a barren desert.

What good is an empty fortress,

Or an empty ship, a ship without people?

TIRESIAS. If evil seems like good to a person . . .

CHORUS. Curse!

TIRESIAS. . . . . calamity is on his path.

CHORUS. Curse!

Curse!

May the ever-present curse finally leave.

(*Pause*)

An insidious

(*Pause*)

An insidious fear

(*Pause*)

An insidious fear shakes us inside

(*Pause*)

I'm wavering . . .

I'm wavering . . .

The Heavens and the Earth are filled with flames of accusation.

The soil is nourished only by blackest fear.

I'm wavering

I'm wavering

I'm wavering

If only the gods would help us . . .

So all words and deeds may

Reach the sacredness
Of divine law.
The laws that were born on Olympus:
That do not sleep or forget,
That do not deteriorate or age
And live on.
The son of arrogance and pride,
The more he is nourished and grows,
The more he sees himself in high places.

TIRESIAS. The penance for this pride will be very difficult! All that has happened and all that will happen is because of you.

CREON. You are the only one who sees it that way in this grand city.

CHORUS. I'm wavering . . .

TIRESIAS. The grand city: Thebes! Don't you see what you have done to this grand city? A city where dead bodies lie in the streets.

CHORUS. Haa! Corpses!

TIRESIAS. A city where funerals are carried out by dogs, scavenging crows, and vultures!

CHORUS. Haa! Dogs!

CREON. Thebes!

CHORUS. I'm wavering!

CREON. Do you hear the things that this insolent man tells me?

CHORUS. I'm wavering!

TIRESIAS. Decaying corpses will be scattered all around. A foul stench will envelop the entire city!

CHORUS. Haa!
Alas!
Corpses torn to pieces!
Haa!
Dogs!
(*Pause*)
The wise oracle has devastated my mind
I can't bring myself to believe it or to deny it.

My mind has gone blank.
I'm wavering. I'm wavering
I'm wavering in the winds of fear!

TIRESIAS. You are searching for the one who buried Polyneices by giving orders and flinging threats!

CHORUS. The one who buried Polyneices
Who!

TIRESIAS. That person is here!

CHORUS. Haa!

CREON. Who?
Speak up!
Tell me, who is this man?

CHORUS. Who?
Speak up!
Tiresias is silent.

CHORUS. Speak up!

CREON. I'm ordering you! Speak up!
Tiresias is silent.

CREON. Are you going against my orders? Speak up! I'm saying speak up!
Tiresias is silent.

CREON. My fellow Thebans!

CHORUS. Ha!
Alas!

CREON. With Olympus as my witness,

CHORUS. Gods!

CREON. I will not let those who rudely mock the state, the laws, and me, get away with it.

TIRESIAS. You'll regret discovering the criminal!

CHORUS. I'm wavering!

CREON. Shut your mouth, fiend!

TIRESIAS. Fury will flood the city! The city will riot!

CHORUS. Haa!

    Alas!

TIRESIAS. You will not be spared the pain.

CHORUS. Gods!

CREON. You are inciting a rebellion!

CHORUS. I'm wavering!

CREON. There is only one penalty for this instigation—and that is
    death!

CHORUS. Haaa!

CREON. And that traitor's body will be pulled from the earth.
    It will be left to the dogs and vultures.

CHORUS. Haaa!

ANTIGONE. No!

CHORUS. Alas!

Blackout.

SECOND STASIMON

(Chorus, Antigone)

CHORUS. Death
    (*Darkness; a pause*)
    Haa!
    (*Darkness; a short pause.*)

ANTIGONE. Death . . .
    (*Pause.*)

CHORUS. . . . They will stone . . .
    . . . They will stone to death . . .
    (*Darkness; a short pause*)
    They will stone to death, for he must have violated the law!
    (*Darkness; a shorter pause*)

The Heavens and the Earth are filled with flames of
    accusation.
The soil is nourished only by blackest fear.
(*Pause*)
I'm wavering!
(*Pause*)
I'm wavering!
(*Pause*)
I'm wavering! I'm wavering! I'm wavering!
(*Pause*)
The wise oracle has devastated my mind.
I . . . I can't bring myself to believe it or to deny it.
My mind has gone blank. I'm at a loss for words
I'm wavering
I'm wavering
I'm wavering in the winds of fear!

Blackout.

EPISODE III
(Creon, Antigone, Ismene, Chorus)

CREON. Fellow Thebans! The instigator has been captured!

    Chorus frozen in silence.

CREON. Who, from now on, would seek news from that crooked
oracle and those black birds? If you ask him, I would have led
Thebes into calamity. The truth is that those worthless predic-
tions were just lies that put treason into words. Not only is
Thebes not being led into calamity but it will now purge itself
of the malice.

    Chorus poses, in silence.

CREON. The traitor who violated law and order and showed no
hesitation when committing this crime . . .

CHORUS. Who?

CREON. . . . was caught, vehemently cursing my orders, where she had buried the corpse that was left for the vultures on my orders.

CHORUS. Ha!
     Who? Who?
     Who dares?
     Who dares to commit such a horrible crime
     Who bears such a flood of fury in their heart
     What maniac would venture into certain, horrible death,
          while aware of the consequences
     Who?

CREON. You! The one with your eyes on the ground!

Antigone is frozen and silent.

CHORUS and ISMENE. Antigone!

CREON. How do you plead?

ANTIGONE. Guilty!

CHORUS. Haaa!

ANTIGONE. I confess. I'm not denying anything.

ISMENE. Ha!

CHORUS. Alas!
     What did you do?
     How could you bring this on yourself?
     How?

CREON. Weren't you aware of my order forbidding it?

ANTIGONE. I was aware!

CHORUS. Antigone! Don't!

ANTIGONE. How could I not be? It has been announced to everyone.

CHORUS. What agony eats at your young, wounded heart?
     Rather than appealing for mercy
     Rather than keeping silent to save yourself
     Rather than keeping silent and staying alive.
     What howl loosens your furious tongue?
     Antigone! Don't!

CREON. So you dared go against my order even though you were aware?

ANTIGONE. It wasn't Zeus who gave the order! Neither has Dike, who rules Hades, burdened us mortals with such an order. And there is no power in your orders that will deem state laws higher than the unwritten eternal laws that protect human honor!

CHORUS. Don't!

CREON. So you know: your defiance will be broken quickly.

ANTIGONE. What will dishearten me? To die, to be killed? In my brief life, I have had as much death as life. I have surrendered my mother, my father, my brothers to it. I know it well.

CHORUS. What agony eats at your young, wounded heart?
Antigone! Don't!

ANTIGONE. Death was always around me. I was only a little child when an embarrassing misfortune took my mother from me with a horrible death. I grew up in the embrace of the cold darkness instead of a mother's warmth.

CHORUS. Huh!

ANTIGONE. For years I've accompanied my unfortunate stateless father in his suffering in exile.

CHORUS. Another calamity?
Is this yet another calamity?

ANTIGONE. I begged them to stop. I cried. But they wouldn't. A dirty war took my brothers from me in a single day.

CHORUS. Huh!

ANTIGONE. I have lived my life with death. I am no stranger to it.

CHORUS. Is this yet another calamity inherited from Oedipus?
(*Pause*)
One does not know how fire burns
Unless one has trod barefoot on flames.
Antigone! Don't!

CREON. The fact that your life is full of agony does not give you the right to disturb the peace of the city in which you were born. Actions have consequences!

CHORUS. Labdacus's descendants have been afflicted with
    catastrophe through the generations.
May the ever-present curse finally leave.

ANTIGONE. To be executed on your order would not pain me, but seeing the naked body of my own brother without a grave, to stand by while his honor is so cruelly trampled would pain me more than anything else.

ISMENE. Haa!

CHORUS. Don't!

CREON. That statement alone is a bare insult to the state's laws. Just thinking it is a crime. You will answer for this!

ISMENE. Alas!

CHORUS. Ismene!

ANTIGONE. Ismene, my sister!

ISMENE. Is there any calamity we inherited from Oedipus which we haven't suffered for in our lives? What a fate!

CHORUS. Labdacus's descendants have been afflicted with
    catastrophe.

ISMENE. Antigone, speak. Did you bury him in spite of the ban?

ANTIGONE. Yes, I buried him whatever the cost may be.

CHORUS. Ha!

CREON. The disobedience of those who live under the rule of another is unacceptable.

CHORUS. The curse! The curse!
Labdacus's descendants have been afflicted with
    catastrophe through the generations.

CREON. This is an uproar that will drag the whole city into calamity. This is open rebellion.

ANTIGONE. Laws should protect the rights of the people, not take them away!

CHORUS. Don't!

ISMENE. Have you gone mad?

ANTIGONE. I loved Polyneices as much as Eteocles, who died with him, and as much as you. What about me putting my own brother in a grave, grieving for him, and showing his dead body the respect he deserves. Is it madness?

CREON. Your grief is scaring this city's people, causing unrest among its citizens. It's not proper to grieve by yelling and screaming like this. This is not respecting the dead: this is defiance!

CHORUS. A storm of fear smothers my soul.
Calamitous clouds pile up.

ISMENE. Knowing that we have not been created to fight the state and the laws of the state is what's proper for us. How could you defy the order? How could you? How?

CHORUS. How?

ANTIGONE. How can you say that? What caused you to set out, bare-foot, for Athens to save our father? What gave you the courage to challenge the state then? Nothing could hold you back from following through on your decisions.

ISMENE. I was trying to save my father's honor. Now I'm trying to save your life. It breaks my heart when I think of what will happen to you. Please don't close the doors of hope by taking this further.

CHORUS. Don't!

ANTIGONE. No!

ISMENE. I beseech you: don't close your mind to my words. Don't get carried away by the wind of the fury that eats at your heart. Don't leave me alone.

CHORUS. One does not know how fire burns
Unless one has trod barefoot on flames.
Antigone! Don't!

ANTIGONE. Enough! For years, I've listened to these words. I'm fed up. For years, you expected me to submit to the catastrophes that buried us. Enough! Why should I be silent when it's possible to change our cursed fate. Or, if we can't change it, at least fight for change. Make our lives worthy by sacrificing them to that end? Enough! Do you expect me to agree that the price for a sin committed by our poor parents in ignorance should be paid for all our lives and for generations?

Chorus poses, in silence.

CREON. Hate has blinded you so much that that you are carelessly relinquishing the peace of this city. I will give you such a punishment that you will drown in your own fury.

ANTIGONE. I'm ready to accept that punishment. That's why I opposed Polyneices's unjust punishment without any hesitation.

ISMENE. What you did on this soil, where you agreed to live as a subject of such a ruler, is forbidden!

ANTIGONE. No! It's a right! No matter the place, it's Polyneices's sacred right. And mine, as well as yours, whether you accept it or not.

CHORUS. I'm wavering . . .

ANTIGONE. It is the right of every human being, whether it's your kin, a stranger, or your enemy.

CREON. That's not what the law says!

CHORUS. I'm wavering . . .

ANTIGONE. I won't observe a law that takes away my most inalienable right.

ISMENE. No, that's a crime!

CHORUS. I'm wavering . . .

ANTIGONE. Yes, but a righteous crime!

CREON. Aaaah!

CHORUS. I'm wavering . . .

ANTIGONE. But if you wish, you can look down on what is honorable.

CHORUS. I'm wavering . . .

ISMENE. I'm not looking down on what is honorable!

CHORUS. I'm wavering . . .

ANTIGONE. Then it's even worse. You don't have the courage to defend something you know is honorable and is your right!

CREON. We'll see how courageous you are when your lungs are burning, from lack of air.

CHORUS. Ha!

ISMENE. Ah, Antigone, my sister! My heart can't bear anymore to see you heading for calamity just like all my other loved ones.

ANTIGONE. Enough! Shut up! Do you think my heart is not crushed as I leave you behind, all alone?

Chorus pauses.

ANTIGONE. No matter what, I prefer an honorable accomplice to a sister who is essentially a ruler's mouthpiece, who expects me to show remorse.

CREON. This stubbornness sounds familiar. Your words reveal you are your father's daughter.

CHORUS. Labdacus's descendants . . .

ISMENE. How can one endure this pain?

CREON. It is clear that rebellion is in your blood!

CHORUS. An everlasting storm is now in her soul.

ANTIGONE. The threat of death does not scare me.

CREON. You'll see when you confront death. You'll regret it a lot!

CHORUS. . . . in a gust of fear!

ISMENE. Alas!

CHORUS. Alas!

CREON. You'll regret it a lot!

ANTIGONE. I protected my brother's rights and my own! If that's why death takes me, I will be happy!

CHORUS. An everlasting storm is now in her soul. I'm wavering . . . I'm wavering in a gust of fear.

CREON. When its reins are held tight, a wild horse quickly calms down.

ANTIGONE. I would rather die than live with those who insult my brother.

ISMENE. I'm begging you!

CHORUS. I'm wavering . . .

CREON. You snake! I have fostered a damned snake, an enemy to my throne, in my own house.

CHORUS. I'm wavering . . .

ANTIGONE. Everybody knows how you acquired that crown and that throne.

ISMENE. Antigone!

CHORUS. Antigone! Don't!

CREON. Oh, so now it has come to this? Will you try to spread discord, just like your cursed father and brother?

CHORUS. I'm wavering . . . I'm wavering . . .

CREON. It's not enough that you rebel against the law, malign my throne?

CHORUS. In a gust of fear.

ANTIGONE. Don't try my patience! Don't make me go on!

CHORUS and ISMENE. Stop!

ANTIGONE. Don't make me tell the people of Thebes what kind of a man you really are!

CHORUS and ISMENE. Antigone, stop!

CREON. Stop flinging threats! Go ahead and talk!

ANTIGONE. Everybody knows what you did to ascend the throne.

CHORUS. Stop!

ISMENE. Don't!

CHORUS. Stop! Don't cross the line!

CREON. What are you trying to say?

ANTIGONE. When calamity befell my father, he wanted to leave. At that time, you kept him in my Thebes to his shame.

CHORUS and ISMENE. Don't!

CREON. I protected him.

ANTIGONE. Lie! And when he wanted to stay in his city, you exiled him from his homeland!

CHORUS and ISMENE. Don't!

CREON. I prevented him from dying in shame because of his sins, of which everyone is aware.

ANTIGONE. That is a lie! You were always burning with desire for power.

CHORUS and ISMENE. Haaa!

ANTIGONE. You, Creon, had your eye on the throne of Thebes.

CHORUS and ISMENE. Haaaa!

ANTIGONE. That wasn't enough for you. You had to drag this city into a dire war by creating bad blood between two brothers. That's how you gained power.

CHORUS and ISMENE. Haaa! Don't!

CREON (*high-pitched scream*). That's a lie!

CHORUS and ISMENE. Alas!

CREON. You are trying to confuse everyone with these words. I loved this country! I served it. I lost a son in that dire war. Even when my heart was burning with the grief over the loss of my son, I didn't forsake this land.

CHORUS. I'm wavering . . .

CREON. But you have turned away from your country. Do you think grand Thebes will accept this evil and vile act without protest?

CHORUS. I'm wavering . . .

CREON. Do you believe that the people of Thebes will heed the slanderous words of a ingrate and forsake their king? You cannot challenge me, Antigone. You are the subject. I am the king. You are the accused. I am the judge. I make the decisions here.

ISMENE. Haaa!

CHORUS. My mind has gone blank.

ANTIGONE. You have even taken away this city's right to mourn. You silenced their cries of agony, let out war cries. It's obvious what you've made of this city: a city strewn with unburied corpses.

ISMENE. Haaa!

CHORUS. My mind has gone blank.

CREON. Do you believe anyone but you will ascribe any value to these delusional lies of yours?

CHORUS. My mind has gone blank.

ANTIGONE. A city where funeral ceremonies are performed by dogs!

CREON. My city wants peace and security, not the curse of such delusions.

CHORUS. My mind has gone blank! My mind has gone blank!

CREON. What city would allow a criminal to disturb its order?

CHORUS. Think!

CREON. What city would allow a person like this woman, who spreads seeds of discord, to bring calamity to their homeland?

CHORUS. My mind has gone blank. I don't know what to say!
I'm wavering in a gust of fear.

CREON. Thebans! This woman has rebelled against order. If this insolence goes unpunished, the order will be turned upside down. And if the order is turned upside down, there will be neither order nor welfare!

Chorus poses silently.

ANTIGONE. Thebans, it's not who's going to teach you what justice is. I am taking what is my right. If what I have done seems like madness to Creon.

ISMENE. Don't!

CHORUS. Don't!

ANTIGONE. May a madman accuse me of madness!

ISMENE. Don't!

CHORUS. Alas!

ANTIGONE. Yes, I committed the crime this man is speaking of.

ISMENE. Haaa!

CHORUS. Haaa!

CREON. Don't you get tired of reiterating your ungratefulness? Aren't you sick of trying my patience?

CHORUS. My mind has gone blank.

ANTIGONE. If it's a crime to out my own brother in a grave,
if it's a crime to respect the dead, then I'm guilty.

ISMENE. I beg you, don't!

CHORUS. Don't!

CREON. Yes, you're guilty! Yes, you have sealed your fate with treason!

ANTIGONE. No punishment that will be given for such a righteous
crime will be hard to bear.

CHORUS. Haa!

CREON. I hate rebels who overestimate themselves, seeing themselves as saints!

CHORUS. I'm wavering . . .

CREON. You have confused rebellion and justice!

CHORUS. I'm wavering . . .

CREON. How are you not ashamed of what you've done? How are
you not embarrassed?

ANTIGONE. I'm not ashamed.
What is there to be ashamed of in returning my brother's
human dignity to him?

ISMENE. Haaa!

CHORUS. I'm wavering . . . I'm wavering . . .

CREON. Wasn't the one who died with him also your own brother?

ANTIGONE. The son of the same mother and the same father!

CREON. By putting this traitor in a grave, aren't you disrespecting
your other brother, who died for his country?

ANTIGONE. The one who died with him was his brother, not his
enemy!

CHORUS. I'm wavering!

CREON. Didn't one try to destroy his homeland, while the other
tried to protect it?

ANTIGONE. A war that set brother against brother ruined this land.

CHORUS. I'm wavering . . . I'm wavering . . .

ISMENE. Alas!

CHORUS. My mind has gone blank.

CREON. He attacked his own homeland.

ANTIGONE. He fought to take back his right to live in his homeland.

CHORUS. My mind has gone blank.

CREON. If he who fights against his own state is not a traitor, what is he?

ANTIGONE. True treason is making brothers fight each other!

CREON. Good and evil are never comparable!

ANTIGONE. Hades gives everyone the same right to be buried!

CHORUS. My mind has gone blank.

CREON. An enemy can never be an ally, even after death!

ANTIGONE. Those who died together, were brothers, not enemies!

CHORUS. My mind has gone blank. I don't know what to say. I'm wavering, in a gust of fear.

CREON. Then you'll go! You'll go join them! I will not submit to anyone's rule as long as I live!

ISMENE. No!

CHORUS. Alas!

ISMENE. Don't!

ANTIGONE. Ismene!

CHORUS. The screams!
What can be done?
How!
How can the flames of revenge be extinguished?
How can the agony of fury be eased?
How?

ISMENE. Creon, you're a sovereign but also a father. She is your son's fiancée. How can you do this to your son?

Chorus poses, in silence.

CREON. So, you drew strength from this criminal and your tongue grew sharp like hers! Look at this ingratitude! Everybody I fostered in my home is against me. But if a king tolerates a revolt among those close to him, others will run wild!

ISMENE. I'm not revolting. I'm begging you!

ANTIGONE. Ismene, don't do it!

Chorus poses silently.

ISMENE. They love each other! Don't do this to them!

CREON. Whoever it might, whether my son's fiancée or my niece . . . This woman was caught red-handed. The fact that she's my relative does not mitigate her treason. Just the opposite: it makes it worse.

ANTIGONE. No!

ISMENE. I'm begging you . . .

Chorus poses silently.

ANTIGONE. Don't!

CHORUS. The screams

CREON. The decision is final!

ISMENE. You can't separate them like this!

CREON. It's not me, but the power of Hades will prevent this union!

ISMENE. No, you can't do this, you can't be that heartless. What's more, when the one who opposes you is clearly in the right then you cannot count on your throne and forsake their life so easily.

CHORUS. Haaa!

ANTIGONE. Ismene!

ISMENE. I'm losing hope. I'm at a loss for words. Can no one hear my pleas?
Haemon, Haemon!

HAEMON. Haaaa!

ANTIGONE. No!

CHORUS. The screams!

CREON (*furious*). Shut up!
Shut up before I lose my temper!

You're insolent!
Don't speak Haemon's name again!
Do you really think my son would choose an instigator over
his father, his kingdom?

ISMENE. Alas!

CHORUS. Alas!

CREON. I don't care if she's my sister's child, I don't care if she's
closest to me of those who worship Zeus under my roof.
Neither this woman nor her sister will avoid their horrible
destiny!

ISMENE. Haaa!

CHORUS. Alas!

ANTIGONE. No!

CREON. Yes, Ismene. I accuse you of being an accomplice!

ISMENE. No!

ANTIGONE. Is it not enough for you to kill me? Will you not find
peace until you have wiped out all Labdacus's descendants,
until you destroy its last scion? Leave Ismene alone!

CHORUS. Labdacus's descendants have been afflicted with
catastrophe through the generations.

CREON. Shut your cursed mouth, insolent woman!

ANTIGONE. What a fate!

ISMENE. What a fate!

CHORUS. . . . through the generations . . .

ANTIGONE. What curse, O gods!

CHORUS. Clouds charged with agony in the sky.
Raging hurricanes unleashed.
The screams!
What can be done?
How!
How can the flames of revenge be extinguished?
How can the agony of fury be eased?
How?

IMAGE 3.4 **Creon, commanding, in one of his signature poses.**
Şerif Erol as Creon.
Eurydice's Cry. Suzuki Theater, Toga, Japan, 2006.
Photograph by Ahmet Elhan (Courtesy: Studio Oyuncuları, Istanbul).

CREON. You, who cries and whines! Do confess that you took part in this crime or do you deny it?

Chorus poses silently.

ISMENE. Yes, I confess!

CHORUS. Alas!

ANTIGONE. No!

ISMENE. I confess! I'm not denying anything.

ANTIGONE. Don't!

CHORUS. Alas!

CREON. You, apparently, have all lost your minds!

CHORUS. Labdacus's descendants have been afflicted with
     catastrophe through the generations.
May the ever-present curse finally leave.

ANTIGONE. Have you gone mad? Dike will forbid you from doing this!

CHORUS. Don't!

ISMENE. No!

CREON. This rebellion has driven you mad. You don't know what you're doing.

ISMENE. I know very well!

ANTIGONE. No!

CHORUS. Don't!

ANTIGONE. It's not like you wanted to do this, and I didn't ask you for help either!

ISMENE. But in the end you were drawn to calamity. I'm coming with you, too.

CHORUS. How can one endure this pain
     How
     How can one bear this grief
     How?
     Labdacus's descendants have been afflicted with
          catastrophe through the generations.
     May the ever-present curse finally leave.

CREON. Shame on you! You're uniting with evil!

ISMENE. I'm not ashamed!

ANTIGONE. I beg you, don't!

ISMENE. No!

CHORUS. The curse!

ANTIGONE. Stop!

ISMENE. No!

CREON. Idiot!

CHORUS. The curse!
    The curse!
    May the ever-present curse finally leave.

ANTIGONE. The gods know who did this!

ISMENE. But the accuser doesn't see a difference!

CHORUS. Gods!

CREON. Apparently, these women have all gone mad!

CHORUS. . . . in a gust of fear.

ANTIGONE. You can't die with me! You can't accept the consequences
    for an action you haven't taken!

CHORUS. . . . in a gust of fear!

ISMENE. Antigone, I beg you, don't deprive me of the honor of
    dying with you. I want to pay my debt to you and my
    brother. I want to share your fate. You can't disregard me like
    this! You can't leave me all alone under this cruelty!

CHORUS. Huh!

ANTIGONE. I beg you, don't!

CHORUS. Don't!

ISMENE. No!

ANTIGONE. If you save yourself I will not be jealous of you! I beg
    you, don't!

CHORUS. Don't!

ISMENE. ENOUGH!

    Chorus poses silently.

IMAGE 3.5 **Chorus members.**
Ahmet Sarıcan and Deniz Karaoğlu as Chorus members,
Eurydice's Cry. Suzuki Theater, Toga, Japan, 2006.
Photograph by Ahmet Elhan (Courtesy: Studio Oyuncuları, Istanbul)

ISMENE. Didn't you want an accomplice? I also share your fate.
(*This is the moment she unites with Antigone.*)

CREON. What you are sharing with her is death! The only thing
you're her accomplice in is death!

CHORUS. Is this a curse or an omen or what?
Is this storm, this hail a punishment from the gods? Clouds
charged with agony in the sky.
Raging hurricanes unleashed.
The screams!
Is this a curse or an omen or what?

ANTIGONE and ISMENE (*they've become a two-person chorus; their poses and
expressions of emotion are exactly the same*). O Thebes! Thebes!

CHORUS. The screams!

CREON. With Zeus as my witness, I will silence you both . . .

ANTIGONE and ISMENE. O Thebes, do you see what I'm suffering and
who's causing it?

CHORUS. If only the gods would help us . . .

CREON. You have united in treason and I will shut your mouths
forever!

CHORUS. So all words and deeds may . . .

ANTIGONE and ISMENE. I have been declared guilty because I respect
the sacred.

CHORUS. . . . reach the sacredness of divine law.

ANTIGONE and ISMENE. O Polyneices!
This my reward for burying you!

CREON. You cannot trick this city with provocations and lies. You've
been declared guilty because you buried a traitor!

ANTIGONE and ISMENE. Gods!

CREON. The gods do not show mercy to the insolent.

CHORUS. If only the gods would help us . . .
So all words and deeds
May reach the sacredness
Of divine law.

ANTIGONE and **ISMENE**. Will no one deliver right to the righteous?

CHORUS. Gods!

CREON. I was a father to you for years. And what have did you do? You incited a riot. You betrayed this city. You betrayed me!

ANTIGONE and **ISMENE**. I wanted justice!

CHORUS. Gods!

CREON. O Thebes! Do you hear this? Do you hear what these rebels are saying?

CHORUS. Gods!

ANTIGONE and **ISMENE**. O Thebes! Will you still remain silent?

CHORUS. Gods, help us!

ANTIGONE and **ISMENE**. Is there no one to resist this cruelty?

CREON. Get out, get out of my sight.

HAEMON. Alas!

CHORUS. Alas!

Blackout.

THIRD STASIMON

(Antigone, Ismene, Chorus)

ANTIGONE. Haaa!

ISMENE. Death . . .

Darkness; a pause.

CHORUS. Haaa!

(*Scream*)

Death . . .

They will stone

They will stone to death

They will drag her away and stone her to death

She must have violated the law for them to drag her away
    and stone her
Which of the gods' laws did she violate
    that they would have her stoned!
(*A moment of darkness*)
My blood rushes in my veins
My breath is a hurricane.
It's approaching! Haaaa!
It's rising!
It's rising!
(*Pause*)
What can be done?
What can be done?
Alas!

Blackout.

EPISODE IV
(Haemon, Creon, Antigone, Ismene, Eurydice, Chorus)

HAEMON. Father!

ALL. Haemon!

HAEMON. I'm your son and you know that I have always followed
    your path.
I have never questioned what you taught me.
    Antigone and Ismene pose silently.

CHORUS. Haaa!

CREON. Do you hear him? Do you hear Haemon?
    Now, these are the words a king would like to hear from his
    subjects, and a father from his son.

ANTIGONE and ISMENE. Alas!

CHORUS. So much more agony awaits Oedipus's daughters
Is there a remedy for this trouble?

HAEMON. Thebans, for a patriot, there is no love that is more
precious than his love for his country.
No lover can make a son forsake his father.

CHORUS. My mind has gone blank!

CREON. Here is a son who think of his father's ally as his own ally,
his enemy as his own enemy.
Haemon, with these words, you have once again shown your
allegiance to this country and what a loyal son you are.

ANTIGONE and ISMENE. Haaa!

CHORUS. A storm of fear smothers my soul!

HAEMON. The gods have given us the greatest blessing: the mind. In
order to see and find the truth, it is enough to stop and think
for a moment.

ANTIGONE and ISMENE. Haemon! Don't!

CREON. You snake! Don't speak my son's name!

CHORUS. I wish I had never seen
I had never heard
If only it were possible to close my ears to the screams
If only it were possible to take refuge in darkness
If only it were possible to be both blind and deaf now.

HAEMON. Father! I know very well how you feel as a sovereign.

ANTIGONE and ISMENE. Don't!

CHORUS. Alas!

CREON. Since the day Megareus was martyred, you have been my
only son. I would never wish sadness upon you. My heart
could never bear your unhappiness. But if the law and my
feelings are in opposition, then my actions as a king must
certainly side with the law. Thus, my son, while I was deciding on this woman's punishment, I was sure that you would
understand.

ANTIGONE and ISMENE. Alas!

CHORUS. So much more agony awaits Oedipus's daughters
> My mind has gone blank!
> My mind has gone blank!
> Is there a remedy for this trouble?

HAEMON. No one can deny the fairness of the decisions made
> through reason.

ANTIGONE and ISMENE. Nobody can reject the obvious!

CHORUS. I wish I had never seen
> I had never heard
> My thoughts are in a jumble.
> Ideas are clashing in my head.
> It's as if my heart will leap from my chest.

HAEMON. Any decision made, any action taken that's deprived of the
> guidance of reason causes calamity.

CREON. These two mad women who, for years, I took into my con-
> fidence and cared for in my own palace . . .

ANTIGONE and ISMENE. If this is madness . . .

CREON. . . . must have lost their minds in ambition and insolence . . .

ANTIGONE and ISMENE. . . . it's an honor to be charged with madness.

CREON. . . . for they have been cursing me, and my sovereignty.
> They have been shooting insults at me and my power by
> letting out unrestrained screams. In front of the whole city,
> they attacked my decisions and the laws of the state.

HAEMON. You could be right . . .

CHORUS. Alas!

ANTIGONE and ISMENE. Haemon! Don't!

HAEMON. But this extreme fury of yours scares me more than
> anything else.

CHORUS. My mind has gone blank!

HAEMON. As a king, above all else you must make sure that your
> decisions and acts are right, that they satisfy both you and
> your people.

CHORUS. My mind has gone blank!

HAEMON. In order to do that, you need a sound and reliable guide. And that is, no doubt, your mind.

CREON. What are you trying to say?

CHORUS. My mind has gone blank!

ANTIGONE and ISMENE. How can one endure this pain?

CHORUS. I
> I
> I
> I'm stunned.
> My mind is foggy and blank
> Ideas clash in my head. I'm wavering
> I'm wavering
> I'm wavering, in a gust of fear.

HAEMON. As a fair sovereign, you need to know which orders you give and which decisions you make are a product of your pride, and which are a product of your mind.

CREON. What are you saying? What are you trying to say?

HAEMON. Where there's rebellion, there's agony, for sure.

CREON. What is this nonsense you're spouting?

ANTIGONE and ISMENE. How to endure this . . .

CHORUS. What exhausts patience
> Is the tiniest straw
> People endure, keep silent
> (*Pause*)
> Endure, keep silent
> (*Pause*)
> Endure . . .
> (*Pause*)
> Endure, keep silent, as if time were never-ending
> But endurance also has its limits.

HAEMON. When those in power shut their ears to pleas and moans of pain, do not hear howls of agony, they are shaken by screams of fury!

CHORUS. Think!

CREON. You are strongly encouraging these women with ambiguous words. Be frank, Haemon, what are you trying to say?

HAEMON. Father, trust the guidance of your power of reason. I beg you to reconsider your decisions for the sake of your country and yourself!

CHORUS. Think!

ANTIGONE and ISMENE. This city is tainted with such malice. Neither Ishtaros nor Phasis could eliminate it!

CHORUS. Is one to come to terms with this and keep silent?
To endure, to wait without moving a muscle?
(*Pause*)
Is it out of respect?
(*Pause*)
Haaa!
Or out of fear, that one waits?
I'm stunned.
My mind is foggy and has gone blank
Ideas clash in my head. I'm wavering
I'm wavering
I'm wavering, in a gust of fear.

CREON. Enough about reason. It's also reason that conspires with evil to commit a crime.

CHORUS. I'm wavering . . .

ANTIGONE and ISMENE. Corpses lay in the streets, spreading disease.

CHORUS. I'm wavering . . .

HAEMON. Father, you hold the highest office.
It's not always possible for you to see everything, to hear what everyone says, and what makes them complain. But I'm among them all the time . . .

CREON. What are you trying to say, Haemon?

CHORUS. I'm wavering . . .

ANTIGONE and ISMENE. Eating carrion has changed the birds' songs.

CHORUS. I'm wavering . . .

ANTIGONE and **ISMENE**. It has changed the dogs' barks.

CHORUS. I'm wavering . . .

CREON. So, listening to those who covet my throne under a pretense of dissatisfaction with the laws, me, and my authority, that is using the power of reason?

CHORUS. Ideas clash in my head.
I'm wavering, in a gust of fear

CREON. Or is it to heed and respect traitors and instigators?

ANTIGONE and **ISMENE**. Lifeless bodies lay in streets.

CHORUS. I'm wavering . . . I'm wavering . . .

HAEMON. I'm not talking about traitors, instigators. I'm talking about your people.

CHORUS. I'm wavering
I'm wavering . . .

CREON. So now I will learn how to govern the state from the people?

ANTIGONE and **ISMENE**. Women are wailing their agony in temples!

CHORUS. I'm wavering . . .

CREON. If those who constantly complain and whine, ignorant of the responsibilities of governing a state and the weight on the shoulders of a king, were in my place they wouldn't last a single day.

HAEMON. Authority has its privileges as well as its hardships.
You hold the law in your hands, you may impose sentences with a nod, but if you don't heed those around you,
you will be alone.

CHORUS. Think!

ANTIGONE and **ISMENE**. You cannot ignore their pleas.

CREON. Should I heed grifters who scheme behind my back and spread discord?

CHORUS. Lamentations for the dead
Will turn into revenge and rise up
Think!

HAEMON. Indirectly expressed dissatisfaction is not necessarily unjust or evil. Of course, any commoner would be scared to give unwelcome news to those power.

ANTIGONE and ISMENE. What kind of cruelty is this?

CHORUS. Is one to come to terms with this and keep silent?
To endure, to wait without moving a muscle?
Is it out of respect?
Or out of fear, that one waits??

CREON. Were the blind, criminals, and rebels not enough? Will I now get a lesson from my own son, too?

HAEMON. It's not like it would be shameful to do so. I am speaking for your sake and for the sake of the entire city. Don't let your rage overcome you. Don't dismiss me right away.

CHORUS. Listen!

CREON (scoffing). Huh!

HAEMON. Heed my words for once!

CHORUS. Listen!

ANTIGONE and ISMENE. Listen to the sound of agony . . .

CREON. Will you keep silent?

HAEMON. Don't insist on your decision and argue that only what you want is right an everything else is wrong. Listen to me!

CHORUS. Listen!

CREON. No!

ANTIGONE and ISMENE. Hear the screams!

CHORUS. Listen!

CREON. When did it become acceptable for a son to say to his father's face, openly and insolently, that he can think better than his father?

CHORUS. Listen!

CREON. Why should I allow anyone to speak to me this a way? Why should I listen to this insolent talk?

HAEMON. Father, don't!

CHORUS. Listen!

CREON. No!

HAEMON. Listen!

CREON. No! I won't listen to you anymore!

CHORUS. Listen!

HAEMON. If you are not willing to listen to me, listen to the sound rising from entire the city!

ANTIGONE and ISMENE. A city where dead bodies lay in the streets.

CHORUS. Listen!

CREON. You're exhausting my patience! You don't know how to talk to your king, or your father!

ANTIGONE and ISMENE. A city where funeral ceremonies are performed by dogs!

CREON. You are shamelessly admonishing me, in front of the whole city to save this woman! She betrayed this city!

ANTIGONE and ISMENE. No!

CREON. Tolerating this crime would be at least as treasonous as committing it.

HAEMON. Hah! Tolerance. What an arrogant word.
Tolerance is different from acknowledging that someone is right.
The fate of the tolerated is up to those who tolerate.
Nobody expects tolerance from you. What is expected from you is justice.

CHORUS. Think!

ANTIGONE and ISMENE. What you're doing is cruelty!

CREON. Are you not ashamed of falling for such a woman and turning your back on your father?

HAEMON. The gods, and the entire city, know that by committing this crime, these women were reclaiming a right you took from them with your arbitrary laws.

CHORUS. Think!

CREON. Are you not ashamed of losing yourself in this cold, this guilty, this dirty embrace, of becoming subordinate to a woman? This woman must have captured your soul for you to diminish yourself like this in front of me.

ANTIGONE and ISMENE. No!

CREON. Do whatever you want, say what you will, even you won't be able to save her from the punishment I have imposed!

CHORUS. Alas!
So much more agony awaits Oedipus's daughters
My mind has gone blank!
My mind has gone blank!
Is there a remedy for this trouble?

HAEMON. Don't you hear how the women of this city secretly wail for these two women? Can't you see how they are inwardly saddened and infuriated by the unjust punishment you have imposed on this woman?

CREON. In this grand city, the only one who sees it that way is you!

ANTIGONE and ISMENE. No!

CHORUS. The more he sees himself in high places.

HAEMON. The whole city sees it this way,
But they're too afraid to say it out loud.
Hear the whispers!

CHORUS. The tyrant, the son of arrogance and pride;
The more he is nourished and grows,
The more he sees himself in high places . . .

HAEMON. They think that this woman deserves a medal of honor for not leaving her brother—who died in a bloody battle of a cursed war—for the starving dogs and vultures, but they're too afraid to say it.

CREON. I don't care what anyone says!

ANTIGONE and ISMENE. You know it as well as I do.

CHORUS. If only the gods would help us!

HAEMON. Apparently, you have intimidated everyone. They keep silent out of fear, not out of respect!

CHORUS. So all words and deeds may . . .

CREON. Are you all trying to drive me insane?
If I deem the law of the state sacred and
respect its regulations, that's tyranny?

CHORUS. . . . reach the sacredness . . .

HAEMON. After a dead person has been deprived of a grave,
violating the eternal law and trampling human pride,
what will be left of the sacredness of state laws?

CHORUS. If only the gods would help us! So all words and deeds may reach the sacredness of divine law.

HAEMON. Can a just punishment come from torturing a human soul, from anguish to human pride?

CHORUS. Think!

CREON. Aaaaah!

HAEMON. You constantly prattle on about the promises you made to this city, about law, about justice. Can a dead body comprehend a punishment imposed on it?
You do not seek justice and order. You're not punishing Polyneices,
You're using his corpse to intimidate the entire city.
This is cruelty, not justice!

CHORUS. Think!

ANTIGONE and ISMENE. My patience is running out!

CHORUS. Think!

CREON. Haemon, don't you see, don't you hear the insolence of these women who are flinging insults at me instead of remorsefully groveling for forgiveness at my feet?
If this isn't rebellion, what is it? If this isn't a crime, what is it?

ANTIGONE and ISMENE. No!

CHORUS. Huh! Huh!

HAEMON. You hear only them, but the entire city says no! These women don't deserve death! If you sentence everyone who doesn't think like you to execution, soon you'll be reigning over a barren desert, not a state!

CHORUS (*very loudly*). Creon, think!
It's better to rule over people than a barren desert.
What good is an empty fortress,
Or an empty ship, a ship without people?

CREON. You ignore the law for the sake of saving these women!

HAEMON. If a law has become the guardian of cruelty instead of justice it should be cut off and thrown away like a rotten limb!

Chorus assumes a series of violent poses.

CREON. Shame on you! You're submitting to a woman!

HAEMON. No! I am not ashamed!

ANTIGONE and ISMENE. O Thebes! Thebes!

CHORUS. The screams!

CREON. Shame on you! You're uniting with evil!

HAEMON. No! If I have disobeyed you just because I love this woman, I would lose only a father. I disobey you because submitting to cruelty would rob me of my human honor.

CREON. So you're also turning your back on me. You're also joining this rebellion.
O Zeus! Why is this happening to me?

CHORUS. The screams!

CREON. Whatever you do, you'll never marry that woman in this world!

ANTIGONE and ISMENE. Gods!

CHORUS. Alas!

HAEMON. All right! Kill them! But others will die with them as well!

CREON. O gods, damn the insolent daughters of the cursed lineage!

ANTIGONE and ISMENE. O Thebes, do you hear these heartless curses?

CHORUS. Alas!

CREON. Damn it!

ANTIGONE and ISMENE. O gods! Do you see?

HAEMON. If there remains anyone who would not object to your madness, then commit this murder with them.

CHORUS. I can't take it anymore . . .

CREON. Has your hatred of me blinded you so completely?
    This isn't murder, it's justice!
    You cannot stop me!

HAEMON. And you can't stop me! I will not be by your side as you commit this murder!

CREON. You will be, Haemon!

HAEMON. No!

CREON. You will be!

ANTIGONE and ISMENE. Alas!

CHORUS. I can't take it anymore . . .

CREON. I will kill these women in front of you.

ANTIGONE and ISMENE. Alas!

CHORUS. Alas! I can't take it anymore
    I can't take it anymore . . .

HAEMON. All right!
    I will be by their side when they are killed, but then you will never see my face again!

CREON. Haemon!

HAEMON. No!

CREON. Stop!

ANTIGONE and ISMENE. Alas!

CHORUS. Alas!

CREON. Haemon, my son, your brother was a casualty of the ambition of these women's crazed brothers, of the curse of a cursed lineage.
    You can't turn your back on me and leave while the pain of Megareus's death is still fresh!

HAEMON. Father, don't!

Chorus performs a quick twitch.

CREON. My shattered heart still aches with the grief of losing a
child. You can't you leave me, too!

HAEMON. Father, I'm warning you, don't do this!

Chorus performs two quick twitches.

CREON. I can see your hatred for me, but don't you have any respect
for Megareus, who fought and died heroically to defend his
city? For the memory of your brother, who loved you more
than his own life?

HAEMON. How can you sink so low?

CREON. Haemon!

CHORUS. Ha!

HAEMON. Aren't you ashamed to make me suffer by bringing
up my brother, rubbing salt into my bleeding wound,
in a situation like this?

CREON. Haemon, my son!

CHORUS. Ha!

ANTIGONE and ISMENE. I can't take it any longer . . . .

CHORUS. I can't take it anymore
I can't take it anymore
I can't take it anymore . . . I can hardly contain it.

HAEMON. You're mourning for him. You say you lost him in war.
You're shedding tears for him.

CHORUS. Ha!

HAEMON. Was it not you who stuffed him with epic tales for years
and then ceremoniously sent him off to this war?

CREON. No!

ANTIGONE and ISMENE. Gods!

CHORUS. The screams!

HAEMON. Was it not you who created bad blood between
Oedipus's sons?

Polyneices had a right to this land as much as Eteocles. Was it not you who provoked this war by declaring him a traitor?

CREON. No!

CHORUS. Ha!

HAEMON. Was it not you who created an enemy by throwing him out of his homeland in order to legitimize your place in the government? Was it not you who let out battle cries, who really desired this war?

CREON. Haemon!

ANTIGONE and ISMENE. The screams!

CHORUS. I can't take it anymore
He's exhausting my patience
I can't take it any longer, the things I see and hear

HAEMON. Do you have a right to mourn for my brother?

CHORUS. I can't take it anymore . . .

HAEMON. Do you have a right to weep for Megareus?

CHORUS. Haaaa!

HAEMON. For years, my brother and I loved you, respected you, believed your lies. But then what happened? Megareus paid for being the son you wanted with his life. And now you're threatening to kill the woman I love before my eyes. You rub salt into my wounds and you use my love for you and my brother to force me to tarnish my honor. You have even exploited Megareus's death. Committing his body to the ground, you disguised your warmongering with crocodile tears and heroic rhetoric. How can you give yourself the right to mourn him? How can you shed tears for him? I am embarrassed to be your son. I'm embarrassed that you're my father.

CREON. Shut up, shut up already! How can you prohibit a father from mourning his son?

HAEMON. Enough!

CHORUS (*quick pose*). Huh!

HAEMON. I wish neither to hear your voice nor to see your face ever again. Nor do I want your love, for which you've made me pay dearly throughout my entire life. Enough!

CHORUS. Huh! Huh! (*Quick pose*)

CREON. How can you know what it means to be torn between one's love for his homeland and one's love for his child?

CHORUS. Huh! (*Quick pose*)

ANTIGONE, ISMENE and HAEMON. O, tomb! The bridal chamber carved from stone.
There I come, before my time.

CREON. Haemon!

ANTIGONE, ISMENE and HAEMON. O Hades! A cruel hand sends me to you!

CHORUS. I can't take it anymore
I can't take it anymore
I can't take it any longer, the things I see and hear.

ANTIGONE, ISMENE and HAEMON. Come, Death!

CHORUS. The screams!

ANTIGONE, ISMENE and HAEMON. Come, O dark Death! End it already, end it!

Chrorus twitches and moans.

CREON. Haemon! Stop! I'm ordering you! I'm ordering you! I'm telling you to stop!

CHORUS. Alas!
I can hardly contain my bitter words
I'm wavering now in the flames of wrath.
I'm wavering.
I'm wavering
Gods, help us . . . !

CREON. O Zeus!

CHORUS. I'm wavering now in the flames of wrath.
Gods, help us!
Gods!

CREON. O Zeus! Empower my tongue and voice!

CHORUS. Huh!

CREON. Go, go and be ruined! You, the son who deserves every
hatred,
The son I can't bring myself to call "my son,"
The most traitorous child among traitors. Go with the curses I call upon you!

CHORUS. Gods help us

EURYDICE. Haemo-o-o-n!

Blackout.

EXODOS
(Creon, Eurydice, Chorus)

CHORUS. Which law of the gods did she violate that they will drag
her away and stone her to death
I can't take it any longer, the things I see and hear
He's exhausting my patience, the things I listen to
I can't contain my words.
I yearn for
I yearn for
I yearn . . .
(*Pause*)
Is one to come to terms with this and keep silent?
To endure, to wait without moving a muscle?

Eurydice poses in silence.

CHORUS. How does she endure . . .

Eurydice poses in silence.

CHORUS. . . . keep silent?

Eurydice poses in silence.

IMAGE 3.6 **Eurydice in agony at the end of the play.**
Şahika Tekand as Eurydice.
Eurydice's Cry. Suzuki Theater, Toga, Japan, 2006.

Photograph by Ahmet Elhan
(Courtesy: Studio Oyuncuları, Istanbul).

CHORUS. For such a long time in silence . . .
　　　For such a long time . . .
　　　How does she endure
　　　Keep silent, as if time were never-ending
　　　But endurance also has its limits.

EURYDICE. I . . . (*She has been silent long enough that her voice is unfamiliar to her. Her voice surprises her, she keeps silent, she can't continue.*)

CREON. Eurydice!

CHORUS. For such a long time in silence . . .

EURYDICE. I, Eurydice!
　　　Unfortunate Queen of Thebes, whose children have been slaughtered.
　　　I . . . the queen
　　　The miserable, silent voice of this city engulfed in pain.

CHORUS. Huh!

EURYDICE. I speak to all those who haven't heard my voice until now.
　　　To all those who expect me to keep silent . . .

　　　Chorus poses silently.

EURYDICE. From the heart of darkness. After the sun of torture
　　　To all the cities of the world
　　　In the name of all the victims
　　　Damn these lips that have kept silent for years!

CREON. Eurydice, don't, don't do it!

　　　Chorus changes pose.

EURYDICE. I, Eurydice! The woman whose heart has been cleaved
　　　　　by pain, whose main artery has been severed.
　　　The woman who has death on her lips, the taste of blood in
　　　　　her mouth.

　　　Chorus changes pose.

EURYDICE. Off my skin I scrape what was given to me as love.
　　　I take back the life I have borne, the world I gave.
　　　In my loins, I squeeze and suffocate the world I gave life to.

CREON. I beg you!

EURYDICE. I bury it in my womb.
Damn the happiness created by submission!

CREON. Don't!

Chorus changes pose.

EURYDICE. Finally, I get rid of this body that has been complicit in tyranny.
I destroy this battlefield that was once my home.
I set this palace on fire. I set all palaces on fire.

Chorus changes pose.

EURYDICE. I rip my heart out of my chest, and throw myself, too, into this fire.

CREON. I beg you, don't!

EURYDICE. O Hades! The last stop of my miserable life!
I release the echo of my voice into darkness and
I come to you.

Chorus changes pose.

EURYDICE. Damn every day that passed in silence!
Damn every breath inhaled without fury!
Come, Death!

Chorus changes pose.

EURYDICE. Come, silent Death
End it already, end it!

CREON. No!

Chorus's poses unify.

CREON. O Thebes, city of cities, look at me.
I, Creon, the king who has devoted his life to the future of his city.
You owe me your peaceful sleep.
You owe me every carefree breath you take.
How did I end up all alone?
Maybe loneliness is the fate of kings.
But how is it that everyone is gone?

IMAGE 3.7 **The cast takes a bow. The set suggests a city on the verge of collapse.**
Eurydice's Cry. Suzuki Theater, Toga, Japan, 2006.
Photograph by Ahmet Elhan (Courtesy: Studio Oyuncuları, Istanbul).

When did this kingdom become so deserted?
O gods, what have I done that made you forsake me?
Why did you condemn me to this city whose lights have
    disappeared, to this palace whose roof is cracking, to
    this night whose morning will never come?

Blackout.

The End

IMAGE 4.1 **Simay sitting in the park as Oruç approaches.**
Elisa Galvagno as Simay and Fabio Marchisio as Oruç.
For Rent, Asti, Italy, 2007.

Photograph by Diego Beltramo
(*Courtesy: Teatro Stabile di Torino*).

ÖZEN YULA

FOR RENT

CHARACTERS

ADNAN	22. Passionate, determined, callow. Has an unusual past.
SADIK	55 years old. Calm, self-confident, dangerous. Has a relatively large frame.
SİMAY	Claims she is 14. Jaded, but sometimes animated. Always lying, always a stranger.
ORUÇ	25. Wise to the world and can be menacing when he wants to be.
KORHAN	17. Somewhere between handsome and beautiful. Callow, enthusiastic, ridiculous when he "shows off."
FERHAN	25. A cur who does whatever the situation requires.

NOTES ON THE PLAY

For Rent premiered at the Astiteatro festival, co-produced by Asti Teatro and Associazione Teatro Baretti, in the park in front of the Asti train station in Asti, Italy, in July 2007, with the following cast and crew:

Adnan	Lorenzo Iacona
Sadık	Nanni Tormen
Simay	Elisa Galvagno
Oruç	Fabio Marchisio
Korhan	Diego Iannaccone
Ferhan	Paolo Giangrasso
Director	Mauro Avogadro
Assistant Director	Elisa Galvagno
Light Designer	Giancarlo Salvatori
Costume Designer	Ivan Bicego Varengo
Music Curator	Luca Tatti

PLAYWRIGHT'S NOTES ON THE PLAY

The leaps in chronology and the breaks in the play are important for both the director and performers as well as the lighting designer. Especially Scenes 7 and 9, even though they would seem to make more sense as the final scene, occur in the middle of the play. It would be more proper to not switch them.

The break between the Scenes 6 and 7 should be kept very short despite make-up requirements.

FOR RENT
Özen Yula

SCENE 1

A park in one of the cosmopolitan areas of the city. A street is visible at the back. There are trees on the border of the street and the park. Beneath the trees are bushes. There are three benches lined up front, side by side. It is late at night. The weather is cool. The moon has mostly hidden herself behind the clouds. A distant park lamp barely illuminates this corner. Adnan sits on the bench to the far right of the stage. He is smoking. A man in a coat and a hat arrives. It is Sadık. He looks around him carefully. Adnan takes a deep drag from his cigarette. Sadık heads towards its glow. Just as he reaches at the bench, the moon reveals itself from behind the clouds. The full moon illuminates the area.

SADIK. May I sit?

ADNAN (*looks at Sadık indifferently*). Whatever.

SADIK. Thanks.(*Takes a cigarette out of his coat pocket after he sits. Adnan raises the collar of his fake leather jacket. Shivers slightly.*) You cold? (*When Adnan doesn't answer*) Spring's coming. Not much longer . . . If you can hold out a little more . . . (*Chuckles to himself. Adnan continues being nonchalant.*) Got a light?

ADNAN. No.

SADIK. What's that in your hand? An airplane?

ADNAN (*throws his cigarette to the ground and crushes it underfoot*). It crashed!

SADIK (*takes an expensive-looking lighter out of his pocket*). I found it. My silver lighter. In my pocket. (*Lights his cigarette.*)

ADNAN (*the word "silver" has caught his attention. He turns to look at Sadık, this time appraisingly*). What are you doing in a quiet place like this, at this time of the night?

SADIK. It's not really that quiet here. Is this your first time?

ADNAN. For what?

SADIK. Is this the first time you're coming here?

ADNAN (*rolls up one of his pant legs and takes out the cigarette pack that he has placed inside his sock. He takes a cigarette and puts the pack back in his sock. He licks his lips, places the cigarette at the corner of his mouth and speaks in a softer tone*). I suppose you would have a light.

SADIK. Did you get that line from an American movie? (*Holds out the lighter, smiling, and lights the cigarette.*)

ADNAN (*grasps Sadık's hand in both of his hands, caressing the hand and the lighter it holds*). Quiet places like this get dangerous at night.

SADIK (*withdraws his hand and drops the lighter into his pocket*). You're new here.

ADNAN. No . . . not really . . . but I don't hang out here very often.

SADIK. I've never seen you here.

ADNAN. So you do come here often, I guess?

SADIK. I've come here quite a bit.

ADNAN. I guess I've only been here when you weren't around.

SADIK. What's your name?

ADNAN. Oh yes, we haven't introduced ourselves. I'm Adnan! (*Extends his hand.*)

SADIK (*they shake hands for a long time. Sadık begins to smile*). I'm impressed. And my name is Sadık . . . I'm fifty-five . . . You probably can't tell in the dark.

ADNAN (*surprised*). Really? You must be in good shape, then.

SADIK. You don't know the half of it. I'm in great shape.

ADNAN. I'm surprised.

SADIK. It's better you be surprised now than later.

ADNAN. No . . . You don't show it.

SADIK. I'll show it when the time comes. How old are you?

ADNAN. Twenty-five.

SADIK (*withdraws his hand and peers at Adnan carefully*). Oh yeah? Come on.

ADNAN. Twenty-five. Really.

SADIK. Come on!

ADNAN. Well, I could go as low as twenty-two, just because you're cute. (*Smiles.*)

SADIK. You look younger than that.

ADNAN. Twenty-two. I'm telling the truth.

SADIK. Good for you. Adnan, where do you live?

ADNAN. I'm not from around here. Just visiting.

SADIK. Where are you from?

ADNAN. Balıkesir.[1]

SADIK (*smiling*). Did you come here to visit relatives?

ADNAN. Yes.

SADIK. Or did you come here to see your friends?

ADNAN. Relatives.

SADIK. So you don't have a place here?

ADNAN. No.

SADIK. That's a shame.

ADNAN. Why?

SADIK. If you had a place, you'd be more comfortable.

ADNAN. If it's comfort you're worried about, Mr. Sadık, it can be pretty comfortable here as well. Like . . . (*Points to the bushes*) there, behind the bushes.

SADIK. Nothing like home for comfort. You scream as much as you want . . . You moan! You groan!

ADNAN. Surely that will happen some day . . . Do you have a place?

SADIK. Yes, I've been there for forty-five years.

ADNAN. Are you from here?

SADIK. Oh yeah. My roots are here . . . (*He laughs.*) Strong roots.

---

1 City of about 250,000 in north-western Turkey.

IMAGE 4.2 **Adnan and Sadık chat after Sadık spots him and introduces himself.**
Lorenzo Iacona as Adnan and Nanni Tormen as Sadık.
For Rent, Asti, Italy, 2007.

Photograph by Diego Beltramo (Courtesy: Teatro Stabile di Torino).

ADNAN. Good. Maybe you'll show me around the city.

SADIK. I think you know this city pretty well.

ADNAN. What makes you say that?

SADIK. I don't think you're visiting. You live here.

ADNAN. That's a stupid assumption!

SADIK. Yet it makes sense, doesn't it? Your house is nearby. You live
with your family. In fact, you're engaged. Or you have a girl-
friend. From the neighborhood. A good lover.

ADNAN (*smiling, a bit surprised*). Could be . . .

SADIK. And . . . you need money!

ADNAN. Everybody needs money.

SADIK. Naturally. I've been in this park so long, there's no way I could forget that everyone has a price.

ADNAN. Of course. If you want something, you gotta pay for it. If you want something good, you gotta pay more.

SADIK (*looking into Adnan's eyes, smiling*). What's your magic number?

ADNAN (*in a hoarse voice*). Eight and a half.

SADIK. I'm asking the price.

ADNAN. Whatever you're willing to pay.

SADIK. You're modest, considering your size.

ADNAN. No . . . If you're pleased, you leave a generous tip. Since you have a place, we'll have no problem moaning and groaning.

SADIK. Do you work somewhere?

ADNAN. I work in a hotel. At the bar. On the top floor.

SADIK. If I asked, you wouldn't tell me the name, would you?

ADNAN. I would. Why wouldn't I?

SADIK. You'd lie. You'd be afraid I'd glom onto you.

ADNAN (*bows his head*). It seems like you know me better than I know myself.

SADIK. Chalk it up to experience, darling.

ADNAN. You're not the only one with experience. (*Puts his hand on his crotch and starts playing with himself.*)

SADIK. We'll see who's more experienced. What's your score?

ADNAN. What do you mean?

SADIK. Jeez! Never mind! You don't actually have a job, do you?

ADNAN. Oh! How many times in a row? I go seven or eight times.

SADIK. Whoa!

ADNAN. Don't you believe me?

SADIK. Very good! We'll get along well. I'll match that score, I'll beat it.

ADNAN. You'll like it!

SADIK. And you'll like the silver lighter, won't you?

ADNAN (*stops playing with himself*). You mean your lighter?

SADIK. Of course. Who knows what else you're hoping to find at the place I'm taking you . . . lover boy.

ADNAN. What the hell are you talking about?

SADIK. I'm saying, who knows what you're hoping to take with you on your way out in a couple of hours.

ADNAN (*suddenly grabs Sadık's hand*). How about you give me the lighter first!

SADIK (*tries to free his hand*). Let go of my hand!

ADNAN (*squeezes harder*). We'll just light a smoke, sweetie. Come on, give me the lighter! Let's see the silver up close.

SADIK (*still trying to pull his hand away*). My hand! Man, you break it and you're screwed.

ADNAN (*grins mischievously*). Now this is really getting out of hand! What if I said, "You're under arrest!?"

SADIK. You're no cop, dude! You're just a bum.

ADNAN. And you're a smartass, Grandpa.

SADIK. People like you aren't cop material, dude. Now, let go of my hand!

ADNAN. Shout all you want. No one will hear you here. First give me the lighter, Daddy. Let's see the silver.

SADIK. Is this your first job?

ADNAN. Whatever. Don't waste your breath. Give me the lighter!

SADIK. You're too hasty. The calmer you are in this job the more you'll make.

ADNAN (*loosens his grip*). What are you talking about?

SADIK (*withdraws his hand*). Look, sweetheart, here's the first lesson: your mind shouldn't be on taking whatever the customer has on him. That's what small-time punks do.

ADNAN. Would you look at this! Check out what Daddy knows and the lessons he has to offer!

SADIK. At this moment, all you'll find on me is a fake silver lighter and so little cash that it'll disappoint you.

ADNAN. Let's see your ID. Give it here.

SADIK. Dude, you're not listening to me at all!

ADNAN. Where the hell is your wallet? (*Reaches for Sadık's inside pocket.*)

SADIK (*opens his inside pocket*). Nothing, see? (*As Adnan checks*) Besides, it would be stupid to rob your customer on your first night at your workplace when you could be working here every night.

ADNAN. Stop giving me advice! . . . First the lighter, then the wallet.

SADIK. Don't push your luck!

ADNAN (*screaming*). Do you think I'm a faggot, buddy? I'm a wretch but I'm not like you, dude!

SADIK. Why are you shouting? If no one can hear us, why are you screaming? You think you'll embarrass me and scare me and take all my money, huh? Everybody here is a wretch, dude.

ADNAN. Shut the hell up!

SADIK. You really have just started this job! You know the ways but you mess it up.

ADNAN. Are you crazy, dude?

SADIK. Ugh, zip it, faggot! (*He takes his hand from his pocket and swings it at Adnan's face.*) Say hello!

Adnan clutches his right cheek with a blood-curdling scream. It is bleeding.

ADNAN. Ouch! God, it hurts!

SADIK. Lesson number one. Mr. Razor. Once you've tasted him, you'll never forget it, baby! I'll introduce you to other unforgettable tastes as well.

While Adnan is on the ground, screaming, Sadık drags him to the bushes behind them. He pulls downs Adnan's pants. Adnan groans, trying to impede him. This time, Sadık slashes the razor at Adnan's right hand. Adnan lets out a terrible cry.

SADIK (*unzipping his pants*). Lesson number two. Mr. Nine-Inches! (*He bends behind Adnan. We see him spit.*) Say hello!

As Sadık thrusts, the stage gets dark.

SCENE 2

Daytime at the same park. It's warm—a beautiful spring day. Simay is sitting on the center bench. She is wearing a high school uniform. She is holding a book, Lolita, and trying to read the first page. Oruç enters wearing a black fake-leather jacket. He looks around, fiddling with the worry beads in his hand. He sits down on the bench to the extreme left. Then begins looking at the girl with interest. He stares at her for a long time. Simay pulls her backpack to her side. Oruç looks carefully at the book's cover and begins to speak the title.

ORUÇ. Lo–li–ta.

SİMAY (*smiling*). Pleased to meet you! I'm Simay.

ORUÇ. No, I mean . . . The name of your book.

SİMAY. Jeez, you're gullible! I was joking.

ORUÇ. Ah . . . nice . . . I like jokes.

SİMAY. Good for you! What's your name?

ORUÇ. Oruç.

SİMAY. How long will it last?

ORUÇ. Huh?

SİMAY. Your *oruç*?[2] . . . (*Giggles*). I'm joking . . . Doesn't it mean "fast?"

ORUÇ. Nah! Apparently, it's the name of an old hero. Oruç Reis. Have you heard of him?

SİMAY. I haven't. What era's he from?

ORUÇ. What do you mean "what era?"

SİMAY. I mean is he from the Independence War? The Victory of Preveza? Or the Battle of Mohács?

---

2 In Turkish, one of the meanings of *oruç* is "fasting" or "abstaining."

ORUÇ. I don't exactly know, but older than those.

SİMAY. Older than the Crusades?

ORUÇ. Jeez, how would I know? By the way, what's your name?

SİMAY. Simay.

ORUÇ. Why don't you tell me what your name means? Does it have to do with the moon?[3]

SİMAY. How should I know? Wait a minute. My late mother named me. She said, "My daughter has hair like gold, it shines like the moon." Moonlight or something like that.

ORUÇ. But you have black hair.

SİMAY. Gee, you're a little thick . . . I'm saying it used to shine in the moonlight. It was golden but as I grew up it got darker. Apparently when I was little my eyes used to be green.

ORUÇ (*leans over and looks*). Did they get that dark later?

SİMAY. Uh-huh. They got darker as I grew up.

ORUÇ. So when you were a baby, you looked European or something?

SİMAY. What'd you think? My father is Italian.

ORUÇ. So, you're, like, half foreign.

SİMAY. Yes!

ORUÇ. Welcome to our country! I'd like to show you our hospitality. We love Europeans very much!

SİMAY. Good for you. What an interesting country!

ORUÇ. Girl, I'm kidding. There's nothing foreign about you.

SİMAY. How old is the girl?

ORUÇ. What the hell are you talking about?

SİMAY. I'm kidding too.

ORUÇ. What the—how old are you?

SİMAY. Fourteen.

ORUÇ. So you'll be a grown-up soon.

SİMAY. I am a grown-up!

---

3 In Turkish, *sim* means "glitter" and *ay* means "moon."

ORUÇ (*laughing*). I was joking . . . I like to make jokes.

SİMAY. I don't really get it, but anyway . . .

ORUÇ. Whatever. I don't get you, either. We just keep talking without understanding each other, like Turkey and Europe.

SİMAY. Do you come here often?

ORUÇ. No.

SİMAY. Don't you have a job?

ORUÇ. I do.

SİMAY. Then what are you doing here at this hour?

ORUÇ. You're a student, aren't you?

SİMAY. Yes.

ORUÇ. What are you doing here at this hour?

SİMAY. Did you blow off work?

ORUÇ. Maybe. What's that you're reading?

SİMAY. A novel.

ORUÇ. I mean, what's it about? What's it like?

SİMAY. Apparently, it tells the story of the love between an old man and a little girl. My literature teacher mentioned it. I was curious, so I bought it.

ORUÇ. Is your literature teacher old?

SİMAY. Yes, but she's a woman.

ORUÇ. What a good book your teacher recommended!

SİMAY. Actually, she didn't! She was giving it as an example of something negative. Something about trash not being literature. That's when she mentioned this book.

ORUÇ. What grade are you in?

SİMAY. I said I'm fourteen. Figure it out.

ORUÇ. Enough already. What's your problem?

SİMAY. What do you do?

ORUÇ. I'm a public servant . . . pubic servant. Depends.

SİMAY. What's that supposed to mean?

ORUÇ. I mean I work in a government office. Boring stuff.

SİMAY. Do you make good money?

ORUÇ (*laughing*). Such lousy questions. How could I be making good money?

SİMAY. What do I know? You're well dressed. You're wearing a leather jacket.

ORUÇ. I make a little money from extra work . . . Are you waiting for someone?

SİMAY. No, I'm just sitting. When I saw the weather was so nice and sunny, I thought I might as well come here. Fresh air makes me feel good. Right now, all my classmates are inside. Stuck in there like sheep.

ORUÇ. But they're learning things!

SİMAY. I'm learning too. Not all learning happens in classrooms.

ORUÇ. Don't you have anyone?

SİMAY. I do! Wait a minute, what are you, some kind of prude? You know, someone who says, "What would your parents think if they knew?"

ORUÇ. It has nothing to do with being a prude, girl.

SİMAY. Not girl. Simay.

ORUÇ. OK, Simay it is! Don't you know this park's a dangerous place? (*Stands up and moves to her bench.*)

SİMAY. No? What's wrong with this park?

ORUÇ. It doesn't look too safe to me. Weird types hang out here.

SİMAY. You mean junkies and stuff? So, what's the harm?

ORUÇ. You might get in trouble.

SİMAY (*feigning fear*). Oh my God. Will they eat me up or something?

ORUÇ. Keep mocking me! There's a lot of jackals around here. When they find fresh meat, they won't let go. There'll be blood. Then you'll see what it means to be surprised. You'll come to your senses when you see blood between your legs.

SİMAY. We're not in a nature documentary. It's the city.

ORUÇ. You want a sesame bagel from that cart? I'm a bit starved.

SİMAY. No. I'll get fat.

ORUÇ. Plumpness looks good on a woman.

SİMAY. I'm still a blossoming girl. I'm just a newborn lamb! You go tell that to some old cow!

ORUÇ. Will you be angry if I buy a bagel?

SİMAY. Are you crazy?

ORUÇ. Hey, watch your mouth, asshole!

SİMAY (*furious*). Why the hell are you bothering me? (*Gradually raises her voice*) Why the hell did you get up from your bench and come over to mine?

ORUÇ (*raising his voice*). So this bench is yours? Did you inherit it from your dad?

SİMAY. I'm sitting here and that's enough! These benches were bought with our taxes.

ORUÇ. You think? As if the state has nothing to do—it buys benches with the taxes you don't pay! Girl, this bench belongs to the government! The state!

SİMAY. You don't say!

ORUÇ. Whose are they, then? Your father, the king's?

SİMAY. My father the king wouldn't put his ass on these benches. This one belongs to the Ministry of Parks and Gardens.

They both freeze for a moment. Then suddenly they start laughing.

ORUÇ. Jeez, we're being retarded, huh?

SİMAY (*as her laughter subsides*). You're a sweet kid. I like you.

ORUÇ. Kid? I'm your daddy!

SİMAY. We'll see!

ORUÇ. Whoa, whoa. What will Miss Simay see?

SİMAY. I think I need to get more life experience.

ORUÇ. So?

SİMAY. Yes, I've decided to get more life experience.

ORUÇ. Good for you!

IMAGE 4.3 **Simay and Oruç flirt shortly after they meet.**
Elisa Galvagno as Simay and Fabio Marchisio as Oruç.
For Rent, Asti, Italy, 2007.

Photograph by Diego Beltramo (Courtesy: Teatro Stabile di Torino).

SİMAY. I think you can help me . . .

ORUÇ. Gladly. Shall we go sightseeing?

SİMAY. Where did you get that idea?

ORUÇ. That's the best way to experience life. You'll know it better when you see penniless people roaming the streets. Then you need to see the lives in the slums. The smell of bars, the smell of laundromats . . . Then the smell of hospitals . . . people on the verge of death. You'll know. You'll experience it.

SİMAY. That's not what I meant.

ORUÇ. I know what you meant. But that's where life's experience lies. Besides, if you want I can take you to all kinds of places. There you can try anything you want—pill, weed, liquid. You'll fly!

SİMAY. All I want . . .

ORUÇ. Stop, I get it. I'll take care of that too.

SİMAY. OK, then. Where will you take care of it?

ORUÇ. A friend has a place. Don't worry. It's a safe place!

SİMAY. How much?

ORUÇ. How much what?

SİMAY. How much money?

ORUÇ. No, if you want money, the deal is off. I can't pay you anything.

SİMAY (*surprised*). Pay me?

ORUÇ. No, your father the king (*laughs*). See, I made a joke.

SİMAY. Yeah, very funny!

ORUÇ. But if you act like this I will ask for money.

SİMAY. You? Of course. How much do you want?

ORUÇ. Don't be ridiculous, girl! So, are you a girl or have you been made a woman?

SİMAY. Yes!

ORUÇ. So you've never done it?

SİMAY. Well, I've come close two or three times but I never went all the way.

ORUÇ. Then I guess we'll be careful.

SİMAY. No, no, with you I go all the way.

ORUÇ. Whoa! All the way? You mean we'll pop your cherry?

SİMAY. Yes! Are you dumb?

ORUÇ. Don't start that again. Watch your mouth!

SİMAY. But you just don't get it.

ORUÇ. I do get it. This is the first time you're doing this.

SİMAY. Bravo!

ORUÇ. Yeah, but, why pick me?

SİMAY. Isn't it your job?

ORUÇ. It is, but I usually work for old people. It'll be the first time I'll do it with a girl who wants to do it for the first time.

SİMAY. Isn't that great? Afterwards we'll have some cake and celebrate.

ORUÇ (*laughs*). Man, can you believe my luck!

SİMAY. What luck is that?

ORUÇ. You know, I don't really work here! I hang out at other spots. This morning I thought I'd wander around a bit as the weather is great. I came here by chance. Fate made me stumble upon you.

SİMAY. Jeez, all this happiness because I'll give it to you?

ORUÇ. Don't start swearing. What do you mean "give?" Be polite.

SİMAY. My apologies! When will you, um, bang me?

ORUÇ. Now. I'll bang your face with the back of my hand, and that'll be it.

SİMAY. I like it rough.

ORUÇ. Girl, this isn't a game.

SİMAY. I know that. When are we going to this friend's place?

ORUÇ. Get up. Let's go. Pack up your *Lolita*.

SİMAY (*throws the book into her backpack*). Come on. Get a bagel if you want. Then let's go. It won't be fun to do it what with all those sesame seeds in your mouth, but what can you do!

ORUÇ. Forget the bagel. Besides, the bagel cart guy's a cop.

SİMAY (*looks offstage, in the direction of the cart*). Sure. And I'm not a girl, I'm a man

Oruç stares at her blankly.

SİMAY (*laughs*). It's a joke!

ORUÇ. Look, I won't pay or anything. I do this for money myself.

SİMAY. OK, I get it! Where's your friend's house?

ORUÇ. Pretty far.

SİMAY (*as she grabs her stuff and starts to walk*). Isn't the weather just beautiful?

ORUÇ. Sure, whatever. What color underwear are you wearing?

SİMAY. Idiot!

ORUÇ. Don't swear. Be polite.

SİMAY (*suddenly grabs Oruç's crotch. Oruç is startled*). Let's take a look at what we'll eat!

ORUÇ. People are looking. Take your hand off!

SİMAY. Sorry, I had glue on my hand. It's stuck. (*Oruç stares blankly.*) It's a joke.

Simay laughs. Stage lights go down.

SCENE 3

Early evening at the same park. It is spring. Ferhan and Korhan sit on a bench on the left of the stage. Ferhan is the better dressed of the two. He has a cellphone in his hand. Everything about him shows that he is experienced. Korhan is a handsome young man but looks poor. Despite all his efforts to be "cool," he looks somewhat childish and ridiculous. Incidents he boasts of end up sounding ludicrous. He has worry beads in his hands. Every now and then he puts them on his wrist, then takes them off again.

FERHAN. Now . . . you can make a lot of money in this business. You're lucky I chose you.

KORHAN. You made me leave the coffee house and brought me here. What's this about, Ferhan?

FERHAN. Dude, use your brain and you'll be fucking rich.

KORHAN. But we're only going to get fucking rich, right? We'll not be fucking people?

FERHAN. Korhan! Dude, you're silly . . . You can't be fucking rich without fucking other people (*Ferhan's phone rings. He signals to Korhan as if to say "one moment." Waits for a few seconds, then answers.*) Hello . . . Yes, yes, it's me. Who is this? . . . Oh, is it you, darling? When did you come back? . . . No, no, I can talk. I'm home. I'm alone . . . I only have my shorts on . . . I missed you a lot. You can tell from the shorts. If only you could see it! . . . Wait . . . Let's not do it now. First, show me the money . . . Yes . . . Tell me where? . . . I know it . . . Ten o'clock. Is this for all night? Well, then be ready to pay for it! . . . OK, honey. Say hi to your wife! (*Hangs up. Shrugs as if to say "what can you do?" Looks at Korhan.*) Look, this comes further down the road. You can then work independently. But there are levels to pass, first. Then you can get into this kind of business without the people here knowing. By the way, keep this between us, OK?

KORHAN. Big talk is fine but you do know what the neighbors are saying, don't you?

FERHAN. Fuck the neighbors. Their mouths all stink from hunger.

KORHAN. Stop right there. You're my boy and all but I won't let you curse the neighborhood. You live there too. Don't shit where you eat!

FERHAN. Dude, what good did the neighbors ever do me? Even my late mother used to look at those dogs and say, "I'd cook my own ass for dinner rather than be indebted to these people."

KORHAN. And my father used to say, "I never let stolen food pass through my kids' stomachs."

FERHAN. Korhan! You're talking out of your ass, dude! That's not how it works. Let me tell you, if it were anyone else in my shoes he'd have broken your nose long ago.

KORHAN. Why's that, bro?

FERHAN. You talk as if I've eaten stolen bread. I've earned every mouthful. Do you think that's easy?

KORHAN. No, bro. Of course, you earned it.

FERHAN. Dude, it'll get dark soon.

KORHAN. So?

FERHAN. So it's time for sucking and fucking.

KORHAN. Bro, this has nothing to do with getting high, right?

FERHAN. What getting high?

KORHAN. You know, being in the sky and so on?

FERHAN. Drugs? No dude! Are you out of your mind? There's too much money in that business. Would they leave that to us? The mafias control all that, dude. And the cheap stuff isn't worth shit. They sell it in the forgotten nooks and corners, but I stay away from that shit. And I have those around me stay away from it as well. If that's what you want, you'd better be careful.

KORHAN. No, brother . . . no such intentions. By the way, what will I do?

FERHAN. How old are you now?

KORHAN. Seventeen.

FERHAN. How long has it been since you've been doing it?

IMAGE 4.4 **Ferhan tries to talk Korhan into joining the business.**
Paolo Giangrasso as Ferhan and Diego Iannaccone as Korhan.
For Rent, Asti, Italy, 2007.
Photograph by Diego Beltramo (Courtesy: Teatro Stabile di Torino).

KORHAN. Doing what?

FERHAN. You know . . . (*Gestures, implying sex.*)

KORHAN (*a little proud*). Oh, that. I was thirteen when I first got some pussy.

FERHAN. Good boy! You started younger than I did. But I bet yours is smaller than mine.

KORHAN (*proud*). That's what you think!

FERHAN. We'll see!

KORHAN. What, I'm supposed to show it to you like a little baby getting circumcised?

FERHAN. No! When we start working we'll see each other's anyway.

KORHAN. What are you saying? We'll do business together?

FERHAN. Yes. I mean, sometimes. If you're up for it. Look, this is how this business works. We join a couple for a threesome. And sometimes the two of us will go with a fag.

KORHAN. What's a threesome, brother?

FERHAN. Oy dude, I mean you're asking questions like a kid. Many married couples are looking for a third person to join them. Either the guy can't get his cock up—he wants to see somebody on top of his wife—or he joins us too and turns around. So it goes . . . If you're better than decent, you'll be rich in no time. Also, when you're leaving their houses you can snatch things. Of course, if you do that you should lay low for a few days. Actually, it's not like anything will happen if you don't. It's not like they're gonna say, "We brought the guy home. He fucked us. And then stole our things."

KORHAN. But I'm not attracted to men!

FERHAN. Well, I'm not either, but you throw some in, you know! Don't worry! You'll see when the time comes! B-u-u-u-t . . .

KORHAN. Ah, here's the catch!

FERHAN. Well done, dude. You're totally off sometimes but you know how to come up with good idioms once in a while.

KORHAN. I do when I need to!

FERHAN. Yes! Now . . .

KORHAN. Is it this hard to say it?

FERHAN. Jeez, you're impatient! How did you wait nine months in your mom's belly?

KORHAN. I can be patient when I need to. I just wanted to make your job easier, brother.

FERHAN. Dude, as with every other business, there are rules. First of all, if you wanna make good money, you gotta last. You need to go in and out for a long time without shooting.

KORHAN. Don't you worry about that! Aysu screams, "Enough! I'm beat! I'll catch fire!" And I still don't stop.

FERHAN. Which Aysu, dude?

KORHAN. You know the baker's wife, that one!

FERHAN. You stud! You screwed Melik's wife?

KORHAN. Pshhh . . . Lots of times. She says, "There are only two paddles like this. The one my husband uses to put bread in the oven, and the one you have." You should see it, she howls like a bellows.

FERHAN. Good for you! But you can't give it away for free anymore!

KORHAN. I don't, anyways. Aysu buys me gifts.

FERHAN. Dude, get it together! You shouldn't do it for the price of two packs of cigarettes. Just wait and see what you'll get here. But you'll have to give me some of it.

KORHAN. Why?

FERHAN. That's how it works here. Dude, I still pay the guy I started out with. Thirty percent of what I make from every job goes to Sadık. There are others like that. If Sadık starts you out, then he gets his share. Either in cash or in some other way!

KORHAN. What, I have to give some to Sadık too?

FERHAN. No, dude. I give some to him. And you give me thirty percent. When you bring a new friend in and start him out, then you take your own thirty percent from him.

KORHAN. What happens if I say "No?"

FERHAN. You can't do business here. You can't even set foot in this park.

KORHAN. If I want to, I can do it somewhere else.

FERHAN. Wherever you do it, you pay whoever's in charge there.

KORHAN. What do you mean "in charge?"

FERHAN. Dude, as the one responsible for you, I'm in charge here. Because I'm the one who's getting you into this business. We make sure you don't get into trouble. You think it's easy? There are perverts, thugs. A thousand kinds of trouble, from acid to blades, all kinds of shit. You give some to whoever's in charge so you get better protection.

KORHAN. Brother, it really is better to go to the coffee shop and play cards! At least there you pay whoever's in charge of the coffee shop and go home. And, of course, whoever loses pays up!

FERHAN. So dude, now you're gonna go rot in a coffee shop? Get it together! Score the guys, score the dolls, then score the money!

KORHAN. Like get the score and get the money! But if they say bad things later in the neighborhood, I'll be upset.

FERHAN. Dude, don't be ridiculous! Neighbors exist to say bad things about everyone. That's their reason for living! And look at me, do you see me getting upset?

KORHAN. But, by now you're . . .

FERHAN. What? By now I'm what?

KORHAN. You've gone a bit overboard.

FERHAN. Dude, don't make me fuck you up! You'll see, once you start making that money, you'll forget the neighbors. You won't give a fuck even if the whole city talks.

KORHAN. Brother, I dig the women, but you know it's tough with men!

FERHAN. Dude, just close your eyes and imagine a woman. Plus, there are some who are more feminine than a lot of women, anyway.

KORHAN. Really . . . Like Gencer's son?

FERHAN. Gencer the carpenter? So, he turned into a fag? What's he up to now?

KORHAN. I heard he's rented a place on the other side of the city and is hosting the neighborhood. The new boys hang out with him.

FERHAN. Well, he had it in him, so it happened. It is not like we'll ever become fags like that.

KORHAN. No way, right?

FERHAN. No, dude! Look at me: Do I look like a fag?

KORHAN. N-o-o-o!

FERHAN. Of course not! Now if you agree to thirty percent, we can pick up the first customers tonight.

KORHAN. What am I gonna do?

FERHAN. Nothing. Just know how to give them the look. That's enough.

KORHAN. What do you mean?

FERHAN. Dude, if you just sit there, once it gets dark, they'll start coming and staring at you attentively. When you return their gaze, they'll come up to you and talk. If you can talk for ten minutes without picking your nose or burping, or farting, you'll even be able to do the customer right here.

KORHAN. Really, it'll work here? In public.

FERHAN. Yeah, it will . . . No one'll care in the dark. You'll go behind the bushes and get it done. Plus, those who come here at that time of the night come here to do that . . . But, as I've said, you need to be a little polite, you need to keep the conversation formal.

KORHAN. It won't work out here!

FERHAN. It will . . . You'll see how it works once you get used to it! It's good to have fresh air . . . The wind caresses you from one side, your customer from the other. Sometimes you get aroused so much you want to do it right there, even before they say, "Let's go." Some are really good at it. You'll see!

KORHAN. I can't do it in out in the open. Someone will see. At the coffee shop they'll start saying "So, Korhan . . . they say you quit poker to get poked in the park." Not cool!

FERHAN. Then go home, dude. Even better. Once you're done and you've got your money, you can snatch some of their stuff. Then we'll have others turn that stuff into cash.

Adnan enters from stage left. He's got deep scars on his right cheek and right hand. In the time that's passed, the cuts have healed but the scars remain. He is wearing stylish casuals. He approaches Ferhan with a smile.

ADNAN. Ferhan, Sadık hasn't shown up yet?

FERHAN (*annoyed at seeing Adnan*). No. He said he'll come late at night.

ADNAN. Did you just meet this guy?

FERHAN. No, he's from my neighborhood. While we were getting laid, he was still in diapers.

Korhan regards Adnan's scars fearfully.

ADNAN. Hey neighbor . . . did you swallow your tongue? Did Sadık cut it off?

KORHAN. What happened to your face?

ADNAN (*with anguish*). Work accident. It happened on the night shift What's your name?

KORHAN. Korhan.

ADNAN. I'm Adnan. (*Offers his hand. Korhan, a little disgusted, takes it. They shake hands.*) Look at that! I'm Adnan, you are Korhan, this is Ferhan. Dude, we're like poetry! (*Laughs. Korhan smiles.*)

FERHAN. How come you're so chatty?

ADNAN. Do you want to shut me up? (*Ferhan glares at him. Adnan smiles.*) Worry has made me chatty. Simay's still not around.

FERHAN. Dude, you'll get yourself in trouble because of that little whore.

ADNAN. She's been missing for two days.

FERHAN. She probably went to her dad.

ADNAN. Come on! Her dad's been pushing up daisies for years.

FERHAN. What do you mean, dude?

KORHAN. It's been a while since her father died.

FERHAN. Shut up! Did I ask you?

ADNAN (*winking at Korhan*). Well, your friend said it right.

FERHAN. Dude, weren't her parents separated? So, she lied about that, too? What a whore! Dude, how did you hook up with this broad?

ADNAN. How do I know, bro? Actually, it's not serious. Like you said, we just hooked up. I can dump her whenever I want.

FERHAN. Is that right?

ADNAN. Hey, I swear.

FERHAN. Love has pulled the wool over your eyes. It'll be hard to dump her. But when Sadık sees you two together during the day and realizes what's going on, I don't know what he'll do!

ADNAN. It's my personal life. Yes, in business we're partners. But why should he interfere with our personal lives?

FERHAN (*laughing*). Those in the public eye can't have personal lives. Don't you know that?

ADNAN. Oy, Ferhan, fuck off.

FERHAN. Dude, it was a joke. Why the attitude? Why the attitude?

ADNAN. Nothing. (*Looking at Korhan*) So what are you up to?

KORHAN. Not much. I might start working at the bakery soon, but you never know.

ADNAN. OK, what do you do in general?

FERHAN. Dude, he's a friend. I brought him here. What's with the interrogation?

ADNAN. I just thought I'd chat for a couple of minutes. Why're you getting upset? Don't worry, you'll get your fifteen percent!

FERHAN (*seeing Korhan look a bit confused*). Thirty percent! I get thirty.

ADNAN. Ha! I see now.

KORHAN. Well, I better get back to the coffee house. The guys'll be waiting. (*Begins to get up.*)

FERHAN. Come on, let's go talk somewhere else!

KORHAN. Bro, really, I should go. I'm sure they need a fourth badly.

FERHAN (*grabs Korhan by the arm*). Dude, they'll find someone else.

KORHAN. They won't get along with anyone else, bro. I've been playing with them for years. We know each other's habits.

FERHAN. You'll be playing bigger games from now on.

KORHAN. I'll play later, Ferhan. But now, I wanna play rummikub. (*Frees his arm from Ferhan's grip.*) I'll see you, brother. (*Walks away without listening.*)

FERHAN. But we'll talk later. (*After Korhan is gone, turns to Adnan*) Screw you! You fucked up a perfect deal!

ADNAN. What did I say?

FERHAN. Well. I was gonna take thirty percent from that guy. That way the fifteen percent I give Sadık would be covered for free.

ADNAN. Well, I got that much.

FERHAN. You got it. What if that bastard got it? Blockhead!

Adnan looks perplexed. Stage lights dim.

SCENE 4

Morning at the park. Simay is sitting on the center bench. She's wearing jeans and a yellow shirt. Over them, a raincoat. Cheap clothes. She's also wearing a pair of cheap sneakers. It's cloudy.

SİMAY. Did you love him? You did . . . Did you believe him? No . . . You wanted to believe him . . . Then why did you sleep with him? . . . I wanted him to love me. I wanted him to love me very much . . . No! . . . I wasn't going to see him again . . . I slept with him, I got rid of it . . . I didn't want anyone to love me . . . Simay, aren't you good at lying? . . . Good job!

. . . You haven't done shit but cry. As soon as we're born they spank us and make us cry. Then we cry for years—that's it! What was the name of the boy? . . . Oruç! . . . No, not him . . . Not the one you slept with . . . The one you didn't sleep with? The one who lit you up inside? . . . Adnan!

Adnan enters. Looks at Simay talking to herself on the bench. Adnan is dressed as before, still wearing the black fake-leather jacket. He approaches Simay from behind and covers her eyes with his hands.

ADNAN. Guess who!

SİMAY. Brad Pitt.

ADNAN (*gets a little upset; then, as he removes his hands*). No, Ayhan Işık![4]

SİMAY. Yeah, people only do that in his movies.

ADNAN. What? Did I do something wrong?

SİMAY. No, not at all. You're so touchy! Besides, I like those old movies. I used to watch them late at night. I like those black-and-white ones . . . Pure . . . Innocent. Hey, if you're Ayhan Işık, I'll be that woman. You know, the one with the beauty mark on her cheek . . . You know, "The Young Lady!"

ADNAN. Belgin Doruk![5]

SİMAY. Yes, Belgin Doruk . . . I'll tell you a secret.

ADNAN. Are you serious or are you fucking with me again?

SİMAY. I'm serious. I won't tell you if you don't want me to.

ADNAN. No, since you felt like it, you might as well tell me. I'll believe you . . . I promise!

SİMAY. Don't tell anyone either. Promise?

ADNAN. Jeez. Every time you make me promise and then tell me some bullshit!

---

4 Ayhan Işık (1929–79) was a film star who made over a hundred movies during the 1950s–70s. He remains an iconic figure in Turkey.

5 Belgin Doruk (1936–95) was another popular film star from the 1950s–70s. She and Ayhan Işık made a popular onscreen couple in the movie series *Küçük Hanımefendi* (The Young Lady).

SİMAY. This time it's true.

ADNAN. Say it then. What is it?

SİMAY. I've done something really bad. (*Pauses. Waits. Adnan looks at her face.*) You're supposed to get curious and say, "And?"

ADNAN And?

SİMAY. It's really bad!

ADNAN. What's this really bad thing?

SİMAY. I . . . fell in love with you!

ADNAN. Stop saying that every other day! I might start to believe it.

SİMAY. Believe it!

ADNAN. How can I believe it? Which of the things you say should I believe?

IMAGE 4.5 **Simay and Adnan fall in love.**

Elisa Galvagno as Simay and Lorenzo Iacona as Adnan.
For Rent, Asti, Italy, 2007.

Photograph by Diego Beltramo (Courtesy: Teatro Stabile di Torino).

SİMAY. Don't believe everything I say. Sometimes I don't believe them myself . . . But believe this. I'm in love with you.

ADNAN. But we haven't even had sex. What kind of love is this?

SİMAY. Well, that's why I'm in love with you. You let me have my heart's desire. You didn't force me into anything like those here or those outside. When I was by your side, no one checked me out with bad intentions.

ADNAN. Well, I've implied a thousand times that I want to sleep with you. You don't get it.

SİMAY. Really, you think I don't get it? Why? Am I stupid?

ADNAN. What, then?

SİMAY. I acted oblivious, dude. I decided to love someone, so I pretended not to get it.

ADNAN. Are you insane?

SİMAY. Yes! But I know you're in love with me too.

ADNAN. Is that so?

SİMAY. Sure. Why else would you constantly try to sleep with me? For people like you, love means sex.

ADNAN. Not at all! That has nothing to do with it. For me, love is your existence.

SİMAY. See, I told you! You're in love with me too!

ADNAN. Yes, I'm in love, I'm in love like a dog. I want to lick you.

SİMAY (*laughing*). Animal . . .

ADNAN. Excuse me?

SİMAY. Adnan . . .

ADNAN. What?

SİMAY. Do you really love me that way?

ADNAN. What way?

SİMAY. Like in those black-and-white movies.

ADNAN. Fuck off!

SİMAY. OK, will you love me that way?

ADNAN. Don't start again.

SİMAY. But I love you that way. As though you love me like in those black-and-white movies. That's why.

ADNAN. You're being silly.

SİMAY (*stands up and takes Adnan's right hand*). Your hand. (*Strokes Adnan's right cheek*) Your cheek . . .

ADNAN (*as if mortified*). Stop it . . . There are people around . . .

SİMAY. I fell in love with these scars . . . They're like a map . . . They're intertwined like the words in my journal . . .

ADNAN. I swear, you're really insane!

SİMAY (*stroking Adnan's cheek*). If only I could fit into this cut on your cheek . . . If only you'd take me wherever you go.

ADNAN. Look—everyone is looking at us. Then you won't have any peace here either.

SİMAY. Nothing will happen to me as long as you're with me. Those jackals will drool, but they can't do shit. (*Continues to stroke Adnan's cheek.*)

ADNAN. Ohhh, I love how you touch my cheek!

SİMAY. Did you know that the moon has two sides? They say one side is always in the dark.

ADNAN. How do you come up with this stuff?

SİMAY. I go to school, dude. I heard it there.

ADNAN. And you're not going to shut up, are you?

SİMAY. Dude, you're the one who's made me into a chatterbox of love.

ADNAN. And your hand . . . Look, as you stroke my cheek like this, I'm getting aroused . . . Come on, let's get away from here for a bit. I'll show you other things to stroke.

SİMAY (*suddenly slaps Adnan on the cheek*). You asshole!

Adnan jumps up. He seems to be in a lot of pain. He is barely able to stop himself from hitting Simay.

ADNAN (*shouts at someone apparently close by*). What the fuck are you laughing at?

SİMAY. Why are you shouting at that guy?

ADNAN. You'll get your turn! What kind of a love is this?

SİMAY. It's its own kind of love, that's all (*Puts her hand on Adnan's cheek and strokes it*) I could have hit you somewhere else too but . . . I couldn't bring myself to do it.

ADNAN. You'd be in trouble if you hit me down there!

SİMAY. Do you have any money?

ADNAN. What do you do with all your money? You make so much. I should really be getting money from you!

SİMAY. I send my mother some money once in a while.

ADNAN. As if she needs it! Didn't you say she was well off? Wait, didn't you say you're only doing this for fun?

SİMAY. Of course she doesn't need it. But I want her to know her daughter has money too, that I don't need the money she keeps holding over me!

ADNAN. And now you need my money, is that it?

SİMAY. Isn't money the most important thing in your life, darling?

ADNAN. No.

SİMAY. Don't lie.

ADNAN (*smiles*). Why, are you the only one who's allowed to lie?

SİMAY. I'm hungry. That's why I'm asking for money.

ADNAN (*takes out a bundle of money from his pocket*). Dollars, euros or Turkish lira?

SİMAY. Got any Brazilian reals?

ADNAN. No. I prefer money I know.

SİMAY. Turkish lira. At least then I'll know how much I owe you.

ADNAN. Fuck owing. Let me take you out to lunch . . . (*Simay looks at Adnan's face as if she can't believe her ears.*) May I? (*Simay's expression changes. She looks as if she is witnessing a miracle.*) I'm hungry too. You and I, we can eat together.

SİMAY. You . . . are asking me out to lunch?

ADNAN. N-o-o-o, we'll get some burgers from right here.

SİMAY. It's the first time anyone's asked me out to lunch.

ADNAN. Yeah, right!

SİMAY. You . . . love me very much.

ADNAN. Yes, fuck it. I love you like a dog. If only you'd give it to me once!

SİMAY. Lunch first!

Adnan looks confused. Stage lights dim.

SCENE 5

A calm dark spring night in the park. There's a new moon in the sky, and a light warm breeze is blowing. Ferhan sits on the center bench. He looks around to see if there's anyone else. Sadık appears behind Ferhan, looks at him and smiles. Then he approaches him slowly from behind. He speaks, disguising his voice.

SADIK. Don't look at my face!

FERHAN (*startled, wonders whether or not to look*). What do you want?

SADIK. I said, don't look.

FERHAN. OK, OK! I'm not looking. What do you want?

SADIK. What's your number?

FERHAN. What number?

SADIK. What can it be? The price. We'll see the other one anyway.

FERHAN. I can't decide before I see you. I don't do this randomly. It matters if the other party is clean. What they want matters.

SADIK. I have AIDS.

FERHAN (*suddenly turns and looks*). Fuck! Sadık, why are you fucking with me?

SADIK (*starts to laugh*). Fuck it, idiot, you bought it!

FERHAN. I knew, dude. Who else could it be at this time of night?

SADIK. Fuck off . . . If you don't look at someone who tells you not to look, your ass is grass. Don't you have any brains at all, dude? It's hard to believe that you've been in this business so long without getting yourself into trouble.

FERHAN. Yet, here I am, right?!

SADIK. Good, good, keep doing it well. Together we'll rake in the money.

FERHAN. I'll bring in a new guy soon.

SADIK. Wow, look at this! So you're becoming a fifteen-percenter yourself. (*Sits down beside Ferhan*) Give me a cigarette! (*Ferhan holds out a cigarette. Sadık takes it and lights it with his silver lighter.*) So, tell me. What's the deal with this new guy?

FERHAN. He's from the neighborhood. The asshole doesn't leave the coffee house but the neighborhood's crazy about him. All the girls come to the window when he passes. Like in a music video.

SADIK. He's a pretty boy, huh? Does he know the deal?

FERHAN. I told him a little. Seems he's open to it. Hes whiny about a couple of things . . . But eventually, when he sees the money he can make, he'll be OK with it.

SADIK. Good. Make him agree as soon as possible!

FERHAN. Let me ask you . . . What do you do with all this money?

SADIK (*suddenly furious*). I shove it up your ass. None of your fucking business. Do I report to you? You're the one who has to report, asshole!

FERHAN. Don't be angry, brother. I was curious—that's all!

SADIK. It's not just your curiosity that'll fuck you but also . . .

FERHAN (*upset*). OK, OK . . . I take it back.

For a while they smoke in silence.

SADIK (*bored, thinks to himself*). I'll be in this business for five more years at most. Who'll take care of me after that? It's been four years since my wife died. The kids split long ago. Not a word from any of them. I'm left all alone. It's only thanks to this job that I didn't start popping pills . . . So, what's next? Am I supposed to wander like those homeless bums on the street?

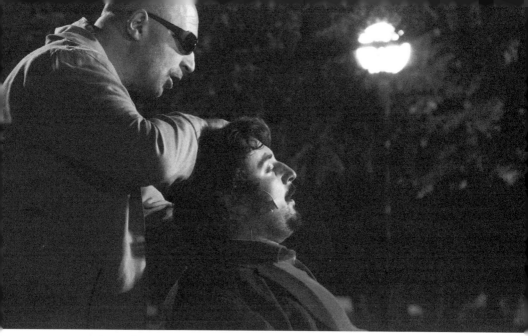

IMAGE 4.6 **Sadık pretends to be someone else and threatens Ferhan, scaring him.**
Nanni Tormen as Sadık and Paolo Giangrasso as Ferhan.
For Rent, Asti, Italy, 2007.
Photograph by Diego Beltramo (Courtesy: Teatro Stabile di Torino).

FERHAN. That's enough, brother. As if we know what'll become of us here.

SADIK. Well, all I want is peace in my old age. In a small town by the sea, a small house, and a garden . . .

FERHAN. Half this city wants to spend their old age like that!

SADIK. I'll be busy with the garden all day. I'll till the soil and plant perennial flowers. Once in a while, I'll cast a fishing line from the calm shore. And in the evenings, dinner with *rakı*[6] and *meze*[7] . . . across from the perennials and the sea . . . mountains and the roses . . . What else would I want! . . . And there'll be some lamb, sizzling on the grill . . .

---

6 Traditional Turkish liquor flavored with anise.
7 An assortment of small appetizer-like dishes eaten as a meal.

FERHAN. So, have the good life!

SADIK. Right, I will!

FERHAN. I'll have that too.

A long silence. They are each in their own world.

SADIK (*suddenly*). I saw this documentary. It was about wild dogs. You know anything about them?

FERHAN. I know of them but not a lot about them.

SADIK. They tear apart gazelles and eat them. They eat and just laze around. When one of them gets old , they drive it out of the pack. Do you know how? They attack it one by one and bite its legs and its body. The old dog tries to get away, in agony, but the wrath of the others takes over. Forgetting its age, it tries to bite back, fighting for its life. But the other dogs are much quicker. The old one can't manage shit. In the end . . . it tries to run away, bleeding all over. It doesn't get far before it falls down and dies.

FERHAN. So?

SADIK. So one should leave before getting killed!

FERHAN. I see . . . (*A brief silence. Ferhan smiles cunningly.*) Sadık, what do you say to this Adnan situation?

SADIK. What's up with the faggot? He looks good with his cuts. (*Laughs.*)

FERHAN. You mean you don't know, brother?

SADIK. What the fuck are you talking about?

FERHAN. Nothing . . .

SADIK. Cut the shit and tell me!

FERHAN. It is . . . there's a young girl.

SADIK. What young girl?

FERHAN. I guess you haven't seen her . . . Of course you wouldn't have. They pick times when you're not around.

SADIK. What the fuck are you saying? Just come out with it!

FERHAN. OK, I'll cut the bullshit. He's pimping her. And he takes all the money himself. He doesn't give any to the girl and you're none the wiser.

SADIK. Which girl is this, man?

FERHAN. Dude, some fourteen-year-old whore. But she's cute.

SADIK. That son of a bitch! Faggot! He'll see when I fuck the shit out of him, I'll fuck the . . .

FERHAN. I just wanted you to know, brother . . . No one has the right to make you look like an idiot.

SADIK (*suddenly grabs Ferhan's crotch and begins to squeeze. It hurts Ferhan a lot*). What the fuck, asshole! Who looks like an idiot?

FERHAN. Aaaah, let me go, brother! Look, they've only been doing this shit for two weeks!

SADIK. And you tell me now! Asshole!

He suddenly loosens his grip. Ferhan crumbles to the ground and begins to throw up. The stage lights dim.

SCENE 6

A spring morning in the park. Birds singing. Adnan sits on the back-rest of the center bench, his feet on the seat. Simay sits on the bench, next to his feet. They are both clad in relatively lightweight clothes.

ADNAN (*looking uneasy*). Why won't you sleep with me? (*Simay takes Adnan's hand in hers. He tries to pull away, she doesn't let go.*) Don't try holding my hand and licking my wound again. I'm not falling for any of that!

SİMAY (*as she kisses Adnan's hand*). But you don't understand me. I love you.

ADNAN. So, what's the problem?

SİMAY. So . . . (*Lets go of Adnan's hand.*) I'll tell you a secret.

ADNAN. Do something else! I've heard enough!

SİMAY. But you won't believe your ears when you hear it!

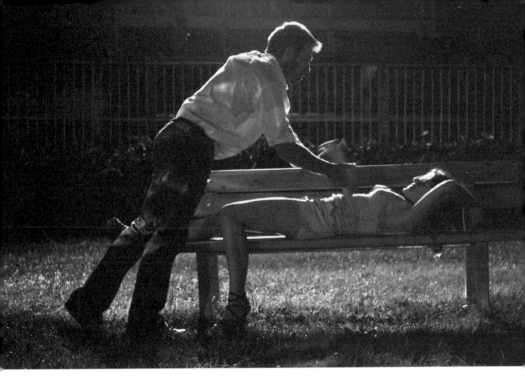

IMAGE 4.7 **Simay and Adnan express their love for each other.**
Elisa Galvagno as Simay and Lorenzo Iacona as Adnan.
For Rent, Asti, Italy, 2007.
Photograph by Diego Beltramo (Courtesy: Teatro Stabile di Torino).

ADNAN *(lights a cigarette)*. Fuck your secret, I say! I've had enough!

SİMAY. Doesn't matter . . . You know my mother, right?

ADNAN. I don't know if that's right or not . . .

SİMAY. C'mon, is there any kid without a mother! I'm telling you I have a mother. But she's a whore too!

ADNAN. Get out of here!

SİMAY. I swear! Look, I'm telling the truth. To be more precise, she was a whore . . . before she died.

ADNAN. Girl, are your parents alive or dead. You gotta pick.

SİMAY. They're both dead. They died the day they stopped loving each other. I swear!

ADNAN. I'm hungry.

SİMAY (*takes Adnan's cigarette and starts to smoke*). I'm not hungry . . . Don't you . . . ever stop loving me!

ADNAN. Jeez!

SİMAY. Promise me!

ADNAN. You're nuts.

SİMAY. You won't stop, right?

ADNAN. Stop what?

SİMAY. Loving me. Promise me . . . Look, I promise you I'll never stop loving you.

Sadık approaches from behind. He sees the two of them. Incredible rage contorts his face. He looks around. When he sees that there are other people present, he decides against approaching them. He exits out the back.

ADNAN. Stop talking nonsense, so we can go and eat something.

SİMAY. I said I'm not hungry . . . How can I make you believe me?

ADNAN. If you're not hungry, what do I care! What's to believe?

SİMAY. No, idiot! How shall I make you believe that I love you?

ADNAN. I'll believe you if you sleep with me.

SİMAY (*suddenly presses the tip of the cigarette into her hand. At the same time, she speaks with difficulty as she groans in pain*). I love you . . . very . . . much . . .

At first, Adnan is puzzled and just stares at her. Suddenly, he realizes what's going on. He takes the cigarette and throws it to the ground. He looks at her hand in horror. At the same time, some gasps and exclamations are heard from the people around.

ADNAN. You're nuts! Everyone's staring at us!

SİMAY. That's very important, isn't it? Everybody's staring at us. You're a coward . . . Coward!

Adnan suddenly pulls up the sleeve of his shirt. He grabs Simay's hand and puts it on his arm. Simay screams both in pain and in amazement. She holds Adnan's arm and brings it close to her face.

SİMAY. My name is written here . . . In a big heart . . .

ADNAN. I wrote it . . . after I heated the needle . . .

SİMAY. You bastard! You love me!

ADNAN (*hugs Simay*). I . . . love . . .

SİMAY. You love me. I know.

> *Adnan suddenly holds Simay's hand and presses his lips on the burnt spot. Simay screams in pain.*

ADNAN. I don't . . . I don't . . . I don't . . .

> *Stage lights dim.*

SCENE 7

Simay sits by herself in the park. She has aged a lot. The lines on her face are obvious. There is grey in her hair and her eyes look very old. She wears a dress too large for her. It could be any time of the day. But during this speech, the sun will set, the moon will rise and day will break once again. Not only days and nights but weeks and months will pass. In fact, it is a transition from the cool of the spring to the heat of the summer. This is the story of an old woman remembering the past and performing a former self.

SİMAY. He loves me . . . Spring, it is the season of love . . . People fall in love in spring . . . So wonderful . . . But love hurts . . . Someone stabs you with an icy sword right here . . . Then they turn that sword here . . . It hurts you . . . You want to go out . . . You want to go and sit under a tree . . . You want to sit there till you hurt less . . . Because this pain will never be completely gone . . . There is always a trace . . . Crying under that tree . . . Thinking about where he is, who he is with . . . Crying yet again . . . You attribute a meaning to every look, every word . . . When a look is just a look . . . And word is just what it is . . . It has no other meaning . . . You would normally understand this, but you just don't when you are in love . . . Even saying "scoundrel" makes you feel good when you are in love . . . It makes you understand where the girls who love sad songs come from . . . I've lived very little on Earth, I barely know its signs . . . But I know enough to know love when I see it . . . I also know that one day love, too, will be over, and that whatever begins will end . . . Love is a sickness, I know . . . It'll pass . . . Like all other sicknesses, it'll leave a virus behind and it will pass . . . I love him very much . . . With his wounds, his mistakes . . . He drives me crazy . . . He goes and sleeps with other men, and women too . . . No, I'm not jealous . . . That's his job . . . What can he do? . . . He has to take money to his kids . . . He's divorced, the kids are with his wife, he covers their expenses . . . And he should . . . After all, he's a father. See, had my father paid for my expenses, would I be like this? Yes, my father's dead, but what if he were alive? . . . I was going to give myself to the man I marry . . . Like it matters if I did? . . . Like some asshole, in some village, didn't take a virgin girl and send her back to her family saying she wasn't a virgin four days later. Like the bastards in her own family didn't kill the girl. Why do families kill their kids? . . . Anyways, this is depressing stuff . . . I love him . . . I want to stay away . . . No, I don't . . . But I should leave him and go home once in a while . . . To take care of my bedridden father . . . Who'll clean him, who'll feed him? . . . This summer I should just take off . . . When you're away, you're rid of this stuff . . . My mother had abandoned us and run away . . . She got rid of us . . . He engraved my name on his arm . . . My love, he loves me so much . . . What does a lover do? . . . They carve a heart into a tree and write two names in it . . . One gets used to pain . . . The tree gets used to its bark being torn, and living with two names in a heart on its body . . . My father gets used to being bedridden . . . My mother to running . . . Adnan to other bodies . . . I am getting used to love . . . Others get used to me . . . I only love him . . . If love is the essence of life, being apart is death . . . Then I die each time we part . . . But I need to go . . . My mother can't get out of bed, she's suffering a lot before death . . . I need to go home every now and then . . . I think I was finished, the day

Adnan was finished . . . You wouldn't believe it if you saw it in a movie . . . Can you believe how in two days I loved him enough for a lifetime? . . . If I lose him one day, I'll have l ost myself, too . . . But if he loses me, he'll have found himself . . . I guess this is the difference between the love of a woman and that of a man . . . It's very cruel, but it's the truth . . . One day I'll sleep with him . . . Just like one of his clients . . . Just like he is one of my clients . . . That's when love will get old . . . The tree will rid itself of its bark . . . The two names carved in the heart will be kept in its essence . . . Then I'll go away from here . . . Night will fall . . . Then it will be morning . . . Then night again . . . I'll kill my bedridden father, my bedridden mother . . . In the name of all the innocent girls killed by the men of their families . . . I'll set the apartment building on fire in the name of decency . . . The flames will be seen by the entire city . . . The smell of the smoke will enter every house . . . All the honorable families will step out onto their balconies and watch what's going on . . . It's not like they did anything but watch for all of history . . . They'll watch from generation to generation . . . Just like they watched those who were killed, kidnapped, went missing, and the performances . . . Those inhaling the smell will say, "In this city there lived a girl who was in love and who was unhappy . . . This is the smell of her house . . . She has decided to get out of here and she is leaving . . . This is the news for that . . . Live for twenty-four hours . . . Goodbye, sweet girl . . . Turkey loves you . . . We will pick up your parents' burnt corpses . . . We'll put them in big black bags and take them to the cemetery . . . Don't you have a family mausoleum? . . . " Then Mommy and Daddy will get the same treatment the homeless get . . . Into a hole . . . I want to lie down under a tree now . . . But not here . . . I want to lie down under a wild tree that grew amidst the greenest grass . . . Let its leaves cover me slowly . . . Just like they covered him . . . This soil, washed with blood, wet and deep, better appreciate the worth of he whom she has taken into her heart . . .

Let her cover my man like love . . . When he was alive, I called
him a bastard . . . But I was in so much love, so much . . . I
was fourteen, I had lived and seen as much as if I were a hundred and four . . . When I used to live in my old city . . . Let
the earth not hurt my man's body . . . I loved him a lot . . .
He was mine, now he is gone . . . Like the sunset . . . But he
won't rise again . . . I wish I had a part of him, a child . . . But
we never slept together . . . Now, I want to let myself into a
deep sleep . . . I was expecting an early death, it didn't happen
. . . I aged in another city . . . Life didn't unfold like a black-
and-white movie . . . This thing that they call life is like the
shadows on the walls in those movies . . . It appears for a
second in the light and then disappears . . . Time has taught
me the grief of shadows . . . I want to sleep away a cruel world
. . . And wake up in a peaceful place . . . (*Sadık appears at the
back. Simay takes a very deep breath*) . . . I want it . . . (*Sadık sits
down beside Simay*) I remember my last day at that park . . .
(*Turns to Sadık and smiles*) That last day that you can never
forget . . . (*Sadık looks at Simay, perplexed.*) Yes . . . I can see
you now . . . And all the suffering souls . . . At this crossroads
. . . I can see.

Sadık looks at Simay in anger. Stage lights dim.

SCENE 8

*The park. An unknown time. Adnan sits on the center bench. He is
wearing his fake-leather jacket. During this monologue the sun will rise
and set and the moon will rise. The monologue will end in moonlight.*

ADNAN. It is cold . . . Even though it's spring already . . . I've always
felt very cold since childhood . . . I was always very cold . . .
Even in the heat of the sun, on summer nights that I would
fall asleep on the slate roof . . . "Şehmus," my mother would
yell, "You'll fall from there, baby." . . . I fell much later . . . In
the big cities . . . Then I fell in love . . . She came into my life

suddenly . . . While I was buried in other troubles, all of a sudden, with her lies and tricks . . . I wanted her to give herself to me just once, she didn't . . . Apparently, what they call love is torture . . . I didn't know it, I found out . . . Many had fallen in love with me before . . . I made fun of them, laughed at them, I amused myself with them . . . Then I ran into this one . . . You know what I wonder the most now? Was her name really Simay? . . . Whatever the heck it was . . . One day, out of the blue, she said, "I didn't know your eyes were green!" . . . I said, "Stop bullshitting again!" . . . "No," she said, "Your eyes are green for this once only." . . . "And?" . . . "See, I lay down on the green grass, apparently I cut my wrist. I wrote your name with my blood on the grass. You are my killer now. That is why your eyes are green, just this once. And me, I've turned green staring into those green eyes." . . . She was still very young, but she was in love . . . She got to learn of love at that age, and she taught it to me too . . . Life sucks . . . I knew that . . . It is not easy . . . The more you know, the more you grow up . . . I got used to life before I got to know death . . . I understood . . . What they called life was ordinary stuff . . . The leaves rustling, the dog barking, the sound of change hitting the ground, the sound of a light switch . . . So life wasn't all that much, I mean it . . . Good money meant a good life once . . . Then I learned seven days could feel like seven minutes . . . Short . . . I used to listen to short stories from clients . . . Life was very important to all of them . . . They all wanted to go somewhere . . . They all believed they would find peace at their destinations . . . A little change, some rest would do them good . . . They were getting very tired . . . Life made them very tired . . . They asked for many things from me, to distract themselves . . . I wanted to bust all their heads . . . My pants had been splattered with the mud of the slums . . . Sometimes I'd get nauseous . . . They stank . . . Their fronts, their behinds stank . . . I wouldn't kiss them . . . I don't know, I just didn't like it . . . It made me nauseous . . . It's not like I didn't try it . . . They immediately put their tongue in your mouth . . . They would start moving it around . . . As if

they want to suck your soul . . . I didn't like it . . . Even if they
paid more . . . Screwing was a dangerous game . . . Whether
you're among the ruins, sleeping under a silky comforter or
waking up in some poor fellow's room . . . Apparently I loved
only her . . . Sometimes . . . There were times when I felt like
those bulls with rings in their noses . . . I mean unhappy . . .
when I thought of her . . . Even though my words can't
express it . . . Some things must change in life . . . One should
be able to change some things . . . When I ran away from
home, after the big migration, I was fourteen . . . Maybe that's
why I fell in love with her . . . Because she said she was fourteen . . . But maybe she was sixteen . . . She lied so much . . .
She believed her lies . . . One day she claimed I had kids, she
wouldn't let go . . . I finally gave in . . . I have kids . . . If it
were possible to go, I'd go too . . . I would lie under a tree
and sleep there . . . In a desolate greenness . . . Now, mine is
a corpse thrown six feet under . . . They looked at the blade
scars on my stomach . . . At the tattoo on my arm . . . They
couldn't guess my story right, not like they'd care if they did
. . . Last, they looked at my neck . . . At my jugular . . . It was
cut with a blade . . . A minor blow . . . From the back . . . The
soil drew all my blood to her depths . . . She was parched . . .
She sucked it so deep down with such desire . . . Here, my
blood fed the roots of these three trees here, they fed on it
. . . As they sent me to the land of the unknown, they jotted
down that my killer was 'unknown' . . . They washed my
corpse and stuck a piece of cotton in my backside . . . "Wow,
look at the cuts on his hand, on his cheek!" one said as he
washed me . . . I heard it . . . Then they buried me in the heart
of the earth . . . I don't have a gravestone . . . But I've fed all
kinds of bugs with my body and my eyes . . . She cries a lot,
she's sad . . . I know it's her! . . . Once there was this girl who
made me suffer . . . Simay, she said her name was, I liked it
. . . I'm a new unknown in the land of the unknown now . . .
All the dead are so lonely and all the mortals are so cruel . . .
We were all about cruelty to our every atom since childhood
. . . If I had lived, I would have been fine with life . . . If it

were possible, I would choose to live . . . To take her and go someplace far . . . To protect her . . . To show her, that my eyes could be green all the time, not just that one time . . . I would have sung her the songs I grew up listening to, I would teach them to her . . . No one taught her songs of any kind . . . That's why she was so unhappy . . . This was the unhappiness of those who couldn't sing even one song . . . It is very crowded underground . . . I look forward to seeing you all . . . in due time.

Adnan smiles. Stage lights dim.

SCENE 9

A summer night in the park. There is light from the full moon. Korhan sits on the bench to the extreme right. It is apparent from his behavior that he has become a man of the trade. He smokes and looks around. Oruç arrives, sits down beside Korhan with a weird smile on his face.

ORUÇ. Hi.

KORHAN. Hi. What are you doing here?

ORUÇ. Same thing as you.

KORHAN (*smiles*). Are you new?

ORUÇ. Uh-huh. You?

KORHAN. It's been about two months or so. What's your name?

ORUÇ. Oruç. Yours?

KORHAN. Korhan.

ORUÇ. Nice name. Does it mean "king of those who fuck?"[8] (*Laughs.*)

KORHAN. It means "I sting like burning coal."[9] You'll get hurt.

ORUÇ. Ah-ha!

KORHAN. Is this your first night?

---

8 In Turkish, *komak* is a variant of *koymak*, which means "to put." *Koymak* is also slang for "to have sex." *Kor* is third person conjugate of *koy*. *Han* means "ruler."
9 *Kor* in Turkish means "burning coal" or "ember."

ORUÇ. No. I used to hang around other places. I came here once before. At daytime. I picked up a young girl. It was my lucky day.

KORHAN. You know the rule here, right?

ORUÇ. What rule is that?

KORHAN. We give thirty percent to the one in charge. So now you'll give me fifteen percent from each job and fifteen percent to the boss. Actually, just give me the thirty percent, I'll pass the boss's share to him.

ORUÇ. But why should I give you fifteen percent? I'll give the boss fifteen percent and I'll give it myself.

KORHAN. No, that's not how it works! Whoever you meet here first, you give him fifteen percent.

IMAGE 4.8 **Oruç asks Korhan for his share.**
Fabio Marchisio as Oruç and Diego Iannaccone as Korhan.
For Rent, Asti, Italy, 2007.

Photograph by Diego Beltramo (Courtesy: Teatro Stabile di Torino).

ORUÇ. Is that so! I'll get you down on the ground and fuck you so hard that you'll give me fifteen percent!

KORHAN. What the fuck are you talking about?

ORUÇ. What are *you* talking about, cutie pants?

They both stand up. Just as they are about to get at each other's throats, Korhan takes a switchblade from his pocket and pops it open. They suddenly stop. Oruç grabs Korhan's hand. The switchblade falls to the ground. They look at each other and suddenly hug.

KORHAN (*laughing*). You bastard! Why would you pull such a prank on me?

ORUÇ (*laughs*). Why did *you*, cutie pie?

KORHAN. Look, don't talk like that again. I don't care if you're a friend, I'll stick the blade in you.

ORUÇ. No, go ahead and stick it in. You'll like it so much you'll want it three more times.

KORHAN. How often have you seen me wanting it three more times?

ORUÇ. Often! Is the money ready?

KORHAN. Haven't made a dime yet. I swear.

ORUÇ (*squeezes the back of Korhan's neck*). Don't lie! Be polite!

KORHAN. Dude, Sadık croaked and we got rid of him. Apparently, Ferhan, that bastard, lifted some stuff from a politician's house, so some asshole took care of him. We got rid of him too! And now we'll have you to deal with! (*Takes out some money from his sock and hands it to Oruç.*)

ORUÇ. Well, if they're dead, I'm here. Every place needs a protector. I've taken over this territory. (*Counts the money and puts it in his pocket.*)

KORHAN. Those before had more mercy. They'd pocket thirty percent by lying and tricking. Now you take almost all the money.

ORUÇ. Well, the new boss makes the old boss look good, honey! Besides, why are you whining? When you're moaning under me you get more than your money's worth. One shares his money with his lover, right?

IMAGE 4.8 **Oruç and Korhan talk about the prospect of a better life.**

Fabio Marchisio as Oruç and Diego Iannaccone as Korhan.
For Rent, Asti, Italy, 2007.

Photograph by Diego Beltramo (Courtesy: Teatro Stabile di Torino).

KORHAN (*feigning anger*). What do you mean "lover," dude? Friend . . . friend!

ORUÇ. That's not what they call it where I come from! Did you give it to me? You did. So then you're my lover.

KORHAN (*teasing*). I don't know what to say. It'll be if it's meant to be. (*They both laugh.*) You know what? I was thinking, let's get out of here.

ORUÇ. Where?

KORHAN. I don't know. Someplace nice. Where we can each get lovers and live comfortably. We'll spend their money without a care.

ORUÇ. Hah, you can forget about that!

KORHAN. Why, dude? Would it be so bad?

ORUÇ. It's not that. To be able to go to places like that, we need to hang out at more posh bars. And that's not possible. The faggots in those places will eat both of us alive. Let's hang around our own neighborhood, with the poor. At least we won't be strangers.

KORHAN. Are you scared?

ORUÇ. Why should you be scared once you know your place? (*Lights a cigarette.*)

KORHAN. Wouldn't you want to go to someplace better together?

ORUÇ. You're too ambitious. It isn't good to be this ambitious.

KORHAN. What ambition are you talking about? Is it ambitious to want a better life?

ORUÇ. Don't get angry right away! We have such beautiful days ahead of us!

KORHAN. Yeah, right. You're talking out of your ass . . .

ORUÇ. You don't want to piss me off. And don't lie to me again when I ask for the money . . . my love!

Suddenly Oruç grabs Korhan by the hair. As he brings the ciga-rette to Korhan's face, the stage lights dim. Korhan is heard screaming in agony in the dark.

SCENE 10

Korhan's scream fades. The park is in darkness. A stifling night after a burning hot summer day. The heat absorbed by the asphalt during the day diffuses in the air. There is very little light. The moon is behind the clouds. Simay appears, barely visible. She is sitting on the center bench. She looks very young. A full backpack is by her side. She has a thin red shawl over her shoulders. She wears a red blouse and red jeans; red shoes, their laces tied around her ankles. Her hands, holding the ends of the shawl, are clasped in her lap. She is going to move very little during this speech. She will stand up as directed.

SİMAY. Distant places always seemed beautiful to me . . . Beautiful, but scary too . . . I used to be intimidated by places I didn't know . . . However, I'm ready now . . . Maybe I was ready then, too . . . I was so young when my parents died, I don't even remember their faces . . . All I remember about my father are his hands . . . Stroking my cheek . . . My grandmother is looking at me . . . I can't leave, I can't go . . . I wouldn't have been able to go . . . Now I'm ready . . . Apparently, I've always been ready . . . Sadık knows . . . He loved Adnan very much too . . . That's what he'd said . . . When he saw me upset, he said, "But I didn't love him as much as you did!" I mean, he didn't love Adnan as much as I loved Adnan . . . I said, "Once he had called me 'Lolita,'" . . . Everything's gone so fast in this world . . . "Now, when you work, you'll pay me as well," said Sadık . . . I said to him, "OK, but I never worked, Adnan used to take care of me," but he didn't believe it . . . I had learned that Adnan was . . . by him . . . He asked me when I would pick up some work . . . "Slowly," he said . . . I said "Tonight!" . . . He gave me a look . . . "The moon will shine on your face," he said . . . "Dress well tonight!" Of course, I did . . . "Look," he said, "I'm giving you a chance. This is a place where men pick up business. You'll be the only woman here!" "I won't let you down!" I said. Then I laughed . . . There was a time in the past when I used to laugh a lot more . . . My grandmother used to say, "My beautiful Suna, when you smile, roses bloom" . . . Then she'd sing an old song but I could never understand the words . . . It didn't matter how hard I tried . . . I have a story . . . But I can't tell it properly . . . Maybe it's because I don't read much, I don't know . . . I fell in love with a man . . . I couldn't express it well . . . There was too much pain . . . I couldn't tell if it hurt more when the body was in pain or the heart was? . . . I am not good at expressing my plight . . . I wouldn't have been able to, even if I were Suna . . . Now

I say, if only he knew my name, but it's too late now . . . I didn't know the body could feel so much pain, and as much as the soul . . . I saw and I watched it in my calmest state. . . I was looking at someone who was suffering very badly . . . You know, one can't die from pain so easily . . . (*A moan is heard from behind, from the bushes.*) Sometimes I hear moans . . . The moans of those who can't manage to die . . . I wonder if that's how Adnan moaned as he was dying . . . I can put the cigarette out on my arm now . . . I wasn't able to do that before, it would hurt too much, I'd start screaming . . . Now only tears fall from my eyes . . . I am screaming inside . . . Once, the first time I felt like reading a book, I stole it, of course . . . But I couldn't finish it . . . There was a boy I used to hook up with . . . He had pronounced the name of the book in a very funny way . . . "Lo–li–ta" . . . Adnan didn't have it together . . . That's what Sadık said . . . (*Moans are heard from behind the bushes. They fade gradually.*) One should be a little tame! What does "tame" mean? I'm hungry . . . If Adnan was here, he'd take me out to dinner . . . How will I find food now at this time of the night? . . . It's time to get on the road . . . Apparently, time also has a soul . . . My teacher said that . . . The soul of time . . . I will leave Adnan here, it hurts . . . I couldn't find his grave . . . (*A very faint moan is heard from behind the bushes. Simay stands up and heads towards them. The moon has come out a little by now. It gets a little brighter.*) Almost done, relax, it'll be over soon! . . . I know it, from my grandmother, it's not that easy to die . . . It hurts a lot . . . If you relax, it will be easier . . . Ah Sadık, why are you so attached to this world? Pain and more pain for one hour . . . Let it go! . . . My grandmother used to say, "The place you call the world is for rent, by owner. When the day comes, we shall vacate, so new tenants can come." . . . Let it go! . . . Do you now understand what Adnan suffered? . . . His suffering probably was shorter . . . His blood must have drained completely . . . He must have gotten cold . . . (*Kicks the body in the back.*) Look, it's better this way . . . (*Comes downstage again. When she bends to get her backpack, she opens her hands. They are drenched in blood. Suddenly she sees her own hands.*) I almost forgot, Sadık . . . (*Throws a long bloody piece of meat towards the back.*) I almost kept a piece of you . . . You might as well go to the other side whole! (*Laughs.*) Once, I was scared of going to faraway places . . . Now, I'm ready . . . *Stage lights don't dim.*

SCENE 10½

Immediately following Scene 10. Same place, same time, same dim lighting.

SİMAY. Far from the smell of my own house . . . (*Adnan enters from the back. He wears the same clothes as in Scene 1. There are no scars on his hands and cheek. He comes forward and sits on the bench to the extreme right. He has a cigarette in his hand. He smokes, calmly.*) I'm now ready for the smells of other rooms, other houses . . . To go to unknown lands . . .

As Simay takes her bag and exits. As she leaves, a man in a coat and a hat arrives. It is Sadık. He looks around him carefully. Adnan takes a deep drag from his cigarette. Sadık heads towards its glow. Just as he reaches at the bench, the moon reveals itself from behind the clouds. The full moon illuminates the area.

SADIK. May I sit?

ADNAN (*looks at Sadık indifferently*). Whatever.

Stage lights go out.

The End

CHARACTERS

WOMAN

Through the female performer we trace an inner journey. Her memory is our collective memory. Woman's scenes with Man are about relationships. When she is not with Man, we watch her inner journey, her relationship to her memory as well as a woman's relationship with society. Her voice is part of the recording that forms the sound score. She also establishes the relationship of the sound score with the stage.

MAN

Man plays the role of an individualized urban male through most of the play. In his relationship with Woman, he is passive, acting along. Woman talks, he moves. Through him we read the condition of a man in a patriarchal society and the difference between the rural and the urban man.

YOUNG GIRL

This performer/dancer is a character that exists both on stage and in the projected images, providing the transition between the two. She also performs three different characters, each representing a different time. In a way, she is a character created by memory. Sometimes she is quite real (onstage), sometimes she is illusory (in the images). Constantly shifting among three characters with costumes that evoke three different periods, she actually represents the mental journey of Woman. Her relationship with Group's Leader mimics the marriage or the ways of building connections between different cultures.

GROUP OF LOCAL MEN

They represent society, Diyarbakır, and tradition. They always move as a group, yet each has his own acts, words, and attitudes.

GROUP LEADER

Diyarbakır incarnate.

YOUNG VOLUNTEERS

Their life choices are different. Their role is to create different encounters with the other characters of the play.

EMRE KOYUNCUOĞLU

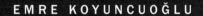

HOME SWEET HOME 1

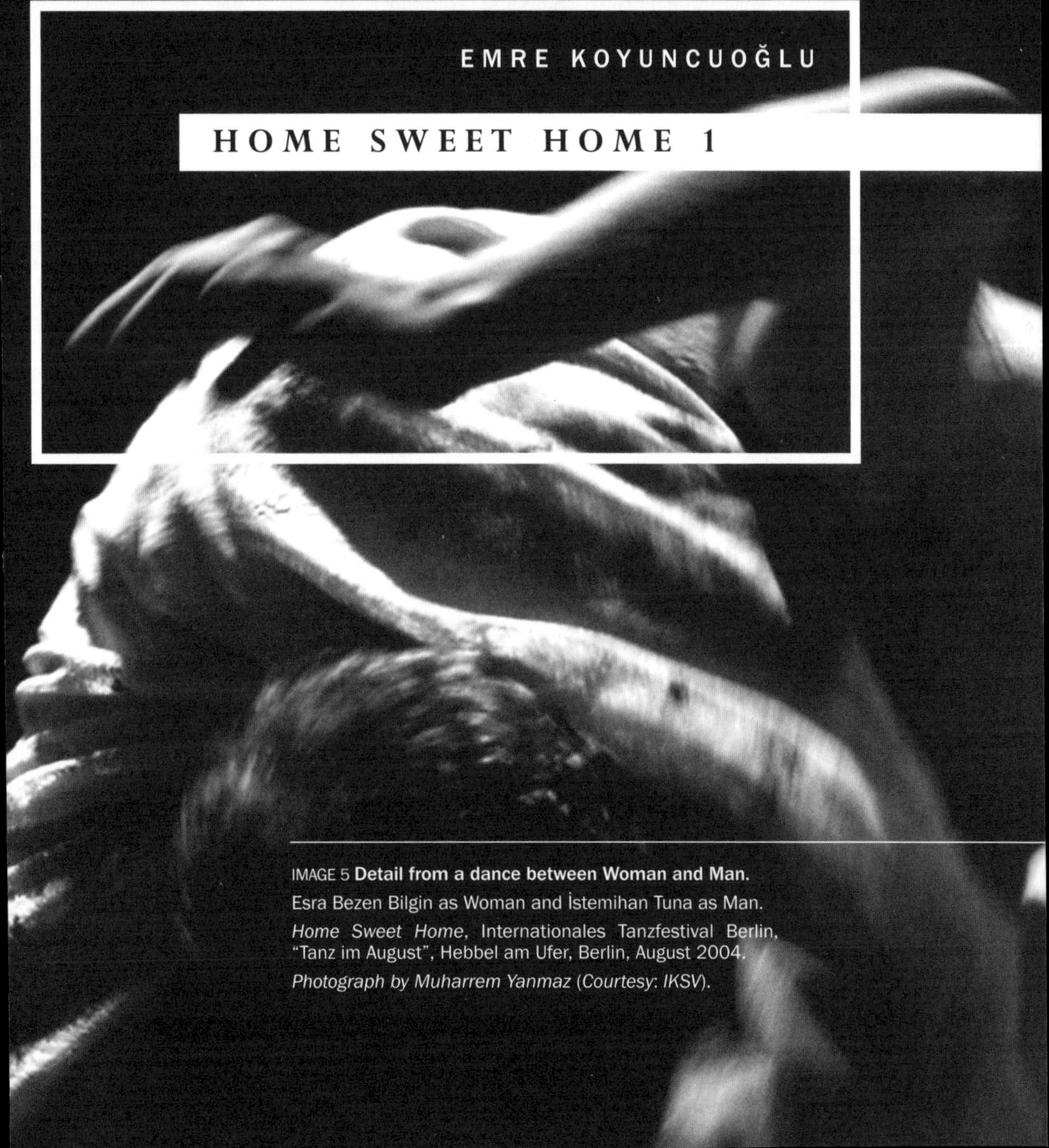

IMAGE 5 **Detail from a dance between Woman and Man.**
Esra Bezen Bilgin as Woman and İstemihan Tuna as Man.
Home Sweet Home, Internationales Tanzfestival Berlin, "Tanz im August", Hebbel am Ufer, Berlin, August 2004.
Photograph by Muharrem Yanmaz (*Courtesy: IKSV*).

Home Sweet Home was co-produced by Kunstenfestival des Artes (Brussels), Tanz im August (Berlin), Diyarbakır Arts Center (Diyarbakır, Turkey), Istanbul Foundation for Culture and Arts and International Istanbul Theater Festival (Istanbul, Turkey), Polyzentral Festival (Hamburg, Germany), and "no Fundo do Fundo" at "a sul 9", Festival Internacional of Portugal.

The original version collected in this volume, *Home Sweet Home 1*, premiered at the Surp Sarkis Church, Diyarbakır, on October 17, 2003. The play was rewritten for different spaces for productions at the Brigittines Chapel in Brussels (2004), Narmanlı Building, Istanbul (2004), Schaubühne am Lehniner Platz, Berlin (2003), and Convento de Santo Antonio, Loulé, Portugal (2005). The Diyarbakır premiere had the following cast and crew:

Woman	Esra Bezen Bilgin
Man	Şafak Uysal
Young Girl	Su Güneş Mıhladız
Other Performers	Hasan Elhakan, Sibel Can, Barış Işık, Sultan Tekin, Mustafa Demir, Ceyhan Demir, Bihter Can, İlker İlkılıç, Murat Şenol, Dengbej Xale Ehmet, Mustafa Demir, Abdullah Yaman, City of Diyarbakır Folk Dances Team, City of Diyarbakır Men's Chorus

Director	Emre Koyuncuoğlu
Sound and Music Design	Çiğdem Borucu
Director of Photography	Aydın Sarıoğlu
Image Editor	Figen Gönülcan
Stage Designer	Elif Özdemir
Light Designer	İzzettin Biçer

Site Consultant	Şeyhmus Biçer
Assistant Director	Emine Özacar
Sound and Music Design Assistant	Koray Başaran
Stage Realization	Öztekin Çaçan
Light Director	Aydın Özdemir,
Image and Sound Director	Mahmut Bozkurt
Stage Managers	Burhanettin Ünlü, İbrahim İçözlü
Assistants	Barış Işık, Zozan Ketenalp

NOTE ON SPACE AND STAGE

The play has been designed for three separate stages built within the same compound.

The play was performed in and around an abandoned, partially demolished building that had initially been constructed and used as an Armenian church, although it was turned into a rice mill during the Republican period (post-1923). The site is in Ali Paşa, a neighborhood of the Suriçi district in Diyarbakır, known to have recieved a huge influx of migrants from villages. Currently it is used as a playground for children and a space for weddings. Local residents, who formed the audience of this production, are used to coming to this place—the backyard of the church is the only open space in a district crowded with narrow streets. It was selected as an appropriate space for the performance because of both its layered historical memory and its relationship to the people of the neighborhood.

STAGE I

The first scene is designed as a prologue for the performance. This prologue takes place on a platform built to face the yard next to the outer wall of the church, in the garden near the main church door. This platform has a 30-degree slope. Dancing and running on a 30-degree slope feels like doing so on nine-inch heels. The platform, hence, is intended to be an impediment to the performers so that they cannot move freely. One must climb, or sometimes slide, in order to move. The choreography of this

IMAGE 5.1 **Surp Sarkis Church, Diyarbakır: site of the *Home Sweet Home* premiere.**

Photograph by Emre Koyuncuoğlu

part of the performance is designed for and rehearsed on a flat surface. Of course, the choreography was tested on the slope prior to the performance but the movements that did not work were *not* changed. The performers' movements are naturally shaped by the slope. The visible strain on the body due to the slope is a desired effect.

STAGE II

A level platform, two feet from the ground, constructed in the apse of the church. To seat the audience, a type of low stools that can be found in tea gardens around Diyarbakır were brought in. The ruined architecte of the church makes this is a frontal stage, resembling an classic Italian stage, temporarily placed slightly above the spectators.

STAGE III

A six feet-by-three feet platform, placed against the inside of the outer wall of the church, in the space that the side door of the church opens onto.

The passage from one space to the other, guided by the performers, highlights the fact that this is a journey that the spectators and performers embark on together: a mental/imaginary/mnemonic journey. Bringing the spectators in from outside through the main door and letting them out through a different door—the side door—is a spatial solution designed to express that in this journey or process, the story of a thought or idea is expressed. (The image of the leeches on the hands of Young Girl in the wedding dress in the videos of the performance provides one-to-one support for this structure. The relationship between Young Girl and the leeches is different in the projections in each scene.) During the performance, thresholds are crossed, doors open other doors, and finally one exits into the same garden but sees it from a different perspective.

NOTE ON STRUCTURE

In the performance, there is no linear structure of time and space; there in no linear plot. The way the scenes are juxtaposed, opening from one to the other, or born out of one another, is like a stream of consciousness. A fantastic, surreal and metaphoric quality is desired for the performance. Everything is open to everything else. There are moments that mirror the stream of consciousness, as scene fragments transform into one another. The totality of these fragments express a certain awareness and the critical/ironic position formed with this awareness. Similarly, the aural and visual language in the performance don't flow in parallel; they are juxtaposed as different realities in order to add dimensions to each other and build the consciousness or critical structure. The text of the performance is a combination of the visual text, the verbal text, the movement text, the music, counter to or juxtaposed with one another—all together, they build the stage text. The fact that different memories and experiences speak and exist in the same space, and that different periods of time exist simultaneously, forces the spectators to think about situations and conditions of coexistence.

The only costumes used in the performance are the three worn by the performer/dancer girl: they represent three generations. Woman was asked to wear a dress, and Man was asked to wear pants and a shirt. The other performers and volunteers were asked to dress as they please, as they did in everyday life. The volunteers were asked to wear what they liked wearing most, that which said "this is me." The Young Girl wears the same costumes onstage and in the stills and videos. Her costumes symbolize certain periods:

1. The "wedding dress," worn by little girls who marched in traditional torchlight processions during the celebrations for the Republic. This tradition has mostly disappeared. Her dress does not look exactly like a wedding dress but more like the dresses little girls wear at weddings today. Her hair is in a bun and adorned with small artificial flowers. In the performance she represents the first generation of the Republican period (my grandmother's era).

2. The "elementary school" costume (black uniform, braided pigtails, red hair ribbon, white collar, black patent-leather shoes, and white socks), represents the second generation, who grew up with the idea of youth idealized by the Republic, educated in Republican doctrines (my mother's era).

3. A headscarf and an ankle-length coat with black rubber shoes. She represents the third generation (my era).

The reason for designating the eras as "my grandmother's era," "my mother's era," and "my own" is a desire to build the story and history, awareness of space, and sharing of time, outside the official language and what has been taught, without logical analysis or linear perception, in a place beyond the officially written and recorded. The play's text is built out of anonymous verbal records. All the dialogue in the performance takes place between pre-recorded voice texts and live performers who are given the freedom to improvise.

The verbal texts are fragments of interview recordings. These interviews were done over the course of a year with people from different parts of the country—they are of different ages, cultures, religions, and they speak different languages. The sounds of the town of Diyarbakır were also recorded. These interviews were then edited into sound clips, and arranged according to certain concepts or themes. A sound text thus developed is, in a way, anonymous, and is the most fundamental text of this performance.

The use of music/voice in the performance is concept-driven. It adds to the critical standpoint of the performance.

NOTE ON THE USE OF VIDEO AND FILM PROJECTION

The rapid transitions of memory in the play is vital—this is the foundation of the dramaturgy of the performance. If the transitions are not fast, the play can mistakenly be thought to have a linear narrative and the performance will seem disjointed. Two kinds of images are used in the performance: images of different spaces and short dance footage or close-ups of Young Girl in different spaces and different costumes.

1. Visuals of different places are used to carry the stage to different spaces and to create a fictional or dreamlike visual space/place of home/homeland. The size of the projections is therefore crucial. Much of the time they cover the whole performance space. The space where the performance takes place already has a memory; it also has an identity. The director intends to show that several realities are lived simultaneously, and that one space has several different times. The projected footage is therefore helpful in building emotional, intellectual, fictional, conceptual spaces.

2. The image of Young Girl, in fact, forms the essential question of the play. The image articulates the transformation that occurs during the journey. First, she appears in an image in her wedding dress. She says something to us. Then, on the second stage (when the spectators go inside), she meets them in person. The fact that the same girl appears in three different

costumes emphasizes the conflict between stagnant reality/ problem and changing conditions/times. The end is also performed by Young Girl (in the wedding dress), who now joins the spectators. However, the entire interrogation and journey is carried out by Woman. She is always a real, flesh-and-blood presence. Young Girl's incarnations are protagonists of Woman's fictional path.

The places in the footage are also in Diyarbakır, among the abandoned ruins of the Sümerbank Carpet Factory, which was built in the early years of the Republic, and was, at the time of the performance, being turned into Sümerbank Park. The scenes in the footage are of, and the choreography inspired by, places in the factory (the cafeteria, stage, manager's office, worker housing, corridors, etc.).

HOME SWEET HOME 1
Emre Koyuncuoğlu

STAGE I. The Church's Garden

SCENE 1

Video footage is projected on the rear wall of the stage. Simultaneously, an audio track is heard.

VIDEO. Young Girl (in the wedding dress, medium close-up) is insistently trying to tell something to the spectators, gesturing excitedly. The spectators can't hear her. The image zooms in on her hands, finally focuses on the leeches on them. Young Girl seems unaware of them; she is single-mindedly trying to convey whatever she is saying. (*Duration: 1 minute, 30 seconds.*)

AUDIO. Instead of Young Girl's voice, we hear fragments of sentences spoken by many people. They talk about migrating and

---

IMAGE 5.2–3 **Young Girl in the wedding dress on video. She gestures to the spectators, trying to be heard. Her hand bleeds because of the leeches. The sound score of interviews plays in the background.**

Su Güneş Mıhladız as Young Girl.
Home Sweet Home 1. Surp Sarkis Church, Diyarbakır, 2003.

Videography by Aydın Sarıoğlu

making a home, accompanied by the sound of bricks being smashed, which sometimes obscures their words.

SCENE 2

The image disappears but the brick-smashing sounds continue. A light comes on in a security booth, which looks newer than everything else, on the left side of the stage.

PERFORMANCE. We see a girl and a young man from among the local volunteers. One stands in front of the booth's window while the other leans against the wall of the booth. They look into the darkness around the booth. They are waiting for something. Young Girl (in the headscarf costume) comes out of the booth and goes into the church.

Woman leans against the outer wall of the church. She waits, looking into the darkness. Once Young Girl passes Woman, Man goes onstage. (*Duration: 1 minute.*)

AUDIO. The sound of bricks smashing, having connected the two scenes, ends when Man enters.

SCENE 3

PERFORMANCE. The choreographed movements of Man and Woman begin in silence. In short, the choreography experiments with finding and seeking one's place. Man and Woman attempt different forms of relationship. All are abandoned. Then the image projection begins.

IMAGE. A still image of Young Girl (in the headscarf costume) hugging a papered wall is projected on the rear wall of the stage. The projection lights up the space and seems to add texture to the wall. (*Duration: 30 seconds.*)

PERFORMANCE. Following this, Man moves in a circular pattern, progressively increasing his speed. Woman murmurs, moving across the stage while acting as though she is trying to memorize something.

IMAGE 5.4 **Dance scene between Woman, fighting oppression, and Man—they struggle until they are breathless.**

Esra Bezen Bilgin as Woman and İstemihan Tuna as Man.
Home Sweet Home. Internationales Tanzfestival Berlin, "Tanz im August", Hebbel am Ufer, Berlin, August 2004.

Photograph by Muharrem Yanmaz (Courtesy: IKSV).

WOMAN. Building a good family makes a person happy. Living without love is like living in a desert. Knowing the joy of sharing is the foundation of the path to peace. Finding one's home, country, is finding peace. Happy kids grow up in happy homes. Beautiful things are nourished by people's hearts. The happy person is the one who shares. The secret of living together happily is being able to hug the other person at even the most difficult moment. The cure for the most critical patient is a hand, reaching out with compassion. The brain of happiness is love, heart its sacrifice, food its sharing . . .

PERFORMANCE. Woman tries to climb the wall. Man tries to help, as though this is the normal thing to do. He lifts her, puts her on his shoulders. The woman is constantly trying to climb as though there is something she wants to reach up there. She goes on until she is out of breath. (*Duration*: *10 minutes*.)

AUDIO. The choreographed movements are watched in silence.

SCENE 4. Interlude

The lights dim gradually. Sound begins. An erbane[1] *sextet goes to the front of the stage and play. They divide the stage while also obscuring it. The performers take their places with the erbane group after they've played for a while. The erbane group and the performers head into the church. They guide the spectators to the location of the second scene.*

STAGE II. The Apse

SCENE 1

After guiding the spectators inside, erbane *group goes to the front of the stage. They form a curtain of sorts in front of the stage. Then, as they slowly leave the stage, they decrease the tempo of the music, but the rhythm of the music is synchronized with Young Girl (in the wedding dress) onstage. The* erbane *beat is mirrored by her body.*

PERFORMANCE. Young Girl continually leaps and strains upwards and in other directions, as if she wants to get out of her own body. She is running away from herself, or maybe she is trying to get away from something or someone we cannot see. She continues leaping until it is hard for her to breathe. This is a performative part. She stops when she gets tired, breathes a few times and starts her "struggle" again. She continues her efforts with stubbornness and persistence. She wears herself out in front of the spectators but breathlessly continues her efforts. When she feels like she cannot

---

1 A traditional Kurdish percussion instrument, similar to a tambourine.

take it any longer, she stops, tries to recover by taking a few deep breaths, and then goes on.

Woman's "Fight with the Self" dance begins. She enters, stage left. She circles the Young Girl with the wedding dress. She tries to reach her or interrupt the struggle. She tries thrice. She realizes she will not be able to do anything, and leaves, stage right. Man enters. He interferes with the struggle. He tries to calm her, restrain her. Young Girl tries to get rid of him with all her might. In fact, she attacks him. Young Girl is very tired but she keeps trying to get rid of him, not giving up. She practically wrestles with Man. Man is also tired. He gives up and leaves. Young Girl (in the wedding dress) is upset that he is leaving, but watches him go.

AUDIO. As Man grabs Young Girl, *dengbej*[2]*–erbane* recordings begin to play. The *dengbej* tells a Kurdish folk tale in song, accompanied by the *erbane* player. The music ends when Man leaves the stage. (*Duration: 1 minute, 30 seconds.*)

SCENE 2

Young Girl (in the wedding dress) leaves the performance space. Woman enters, stage left. Woman acts like she is touring a museum. She is trying to remember something. She looks at the walls, touches them. She has a dialogue with the recorded audio text, improvising, as she walks among the images and voices she has created in the space. As Woman walks around the space, an image of Young Girl (in the elementary school uniform) is projected on the rear wall. It is as if Young Girl is being poured into the space, like the voices. Then, the group of local men enters the space, in single file. They stop in certain places and pose facing the spectators. It is as though the things in Woman's memory have become real. (Duration: 4 minutes.)

IMAGE. Young Girl (in the elementary school costume) has a serious look. Medium close-up still is projected on the entire space. (*Duration: 2 minutes.*)

---

2 A type of traditional Kurdish vocalist.

IMAGE 5.5 **Woman stands on a carpet surrounded by ground meat. In the background is a projected video of Young Girl.**

Esra Bezen Bilgin as Woman.
Home Sweet Home 2. Kunsten Festival des Artes, Brigittines Chapel in Brussels, May 2004.
Photograph by Evrim Altuğ.

AUDIO. Woman is in dialogue:

FIRST-GENERATION WOMAN. . . . there are three castles, one inside the other . . . three castles, one inside the other . . . Actually, the main door is huge . . . You enter, the second door is a little smaller, there is a villa-like place past the third door . . .

THIRD-GENERATION WOMAN. It is now a very strange thing to look to the past . . .

FIRST-GENERATION WOMAN. But, both the one who comes in and the one who does not come in regrets it . . .

THIRD-GENERATION WOMAN. Once the matter of history enters, amnesia also comes in . . .

Image appears.

FIRST-GENERATION WOMAN. We never carried them with us, or if we have, my brother took them . . . he went there, I have gone elsewhere . . . I mean, the memories have been wasted . . .

SECOND-GENERATION MAN. They suffered, they agreed to their fate, and they wouldn't complain . . .

THIRD-GENERATION MAN. My mother suffered the most torment . . .

THIRD-GENERATION WOMAN. I feel a lot better when I remember my dream.

Four of the local men enter the stage. They assume poses facing the spectators. They look like they are in the army, having a picture taken as a memento.

FIRST-GENERATION WOMAN. I knew the addresses, but how could I know that you would ask such questions . . .

SECOND-GENERATION MAN. We came here from a small town in Thessalonica . . . where was that . . . it was on my mind just now, it was just on my mind . . . anyway . . .

THIRD-GENERATION WOMAN. What we did, how we decided to move there . . . I don't even remember making the decision . . .

THIRD-GENERATION MAN. My memory is not very good either . . .

THIRD-GENERATION WOMAN. Strange, somehow my brain erased that moment . . .

THIRD-GENERATION MAN. You know . . . my parents get up, it is very calm . . . I mean it hasn't been calm like that, ever. It is totally silent . . . and then, my mom tells my brother, "Hey, there is something going on, get up," she says . . . they turn the radio on, they hear there has been a military coup!

The video and the images end. Woman is left alone onstage. She focuses on the voices and comments on what they say.

THIRD-GENERATION WOMAN. Just at the time in my life when I feel the most productive, I feel as if my productivity has been restricted . . . it is a very strange thing . . .

SECOND-GENERATION MAN. One of them suffered a lot. My other brother wasn't caught often. He was clever.

THIRD-GENERATION WOMAN. Physically and psychologically, it's a period that's completely open to productivity and giving birth, but it's as if all is closed. Very strange.

SECOND-GENERATION MAN. Then I said, in the '70s, "I'll do scientific research." Everyone laughed. They asked, "What will you do with research?"

THIRD-GENERATION WOMAN. It's as if I'm not allowed to give birth to anything new. So strange . . .

THIRD-GENERATION MAN. Why is peace of mind important to a person? Because they have experienced its absence . . .

SECOND-GENERATION WOMAN. I felt that my father had the apparent authority, and my mom had the hidden authority . . .

THIRD-GENERATION WOMAN. I want to be unashamed when I am walking around . . . not to be ashamed . . . I'm . . . ashamed . . .

FIRST-GENERATION MAN. I mean, we're trying to keep things going around here . . .

FIRST-GENERATION WOMAN. Listen very carefully, I might forget, I might not be able to tell it again . . .

FIRST-GENERATION MAN. The Syriac Orthodox, or in other words, the Aramaics . . .

FIRST-GENERATION MAN. But, before they left, they kissed our Muslim brothers . . .

FIRST-GENERATION MAN. In Istanbul, in Europe, you know . . . scattered . . .

FIRST-GENERATION WOMAN. I mean, that's why I really want to go and see, the image is still in my mind's eye . . . I mean,

I know the house, I would recognize it. If I go, I will see it for real?

SECOND-GENERATION MAN. . . . would have really wanted to see it . . .

FIRST-GENERATION MAN. . . . so that it would be left a memory. . .

FIRST-GENERATION WOMAN. We have many wonderful stories, they go like this . . . Oh, well, sweetheart, this is what happens . . .

Woman is alone on stage and her dialogue with the audio text continues until the end of the text.

SCENE 3

Man enters, stage left. At that very moment Woman leaves, stage right. They don't notice each other. As Man enters, video begins.

VIDEO. Bats, like one often sees in the skies above Diyarbakır. Many bats in flight against a blue background.

The video is projected on the whole stage. Man goes through his choreographed movements (broad, full-bodied circular motions; his body language is the language of "contemporary dance") at the edge of the video image. On the back wall of the stage, a young man, one of the volunteers, carefully sidles from stage left to stage right without losing contact with the wall, as if he is walking on a narrow ledge. They are measuring the space without seeing one another. The volunteer's movement is linear; Man, on the other hand, moves in circles. (*Duration: Maximum 2 minutes.*)

AUDIO. We hear only the pre-recorded sounds of the steps of the "Scorpion Squash" dance, a local folk dance performed by the group of local men. The footfalls of the folk dancers begin at the same time as the video and Man's movements, and two minutes later they stop abruptly when the folk dancers move in in single file to the front of the stage. (*Duration: Maximum 2 minutes.*)

SCENE 4

PERFORMANCE. The folk dancers form a wall at the front of the stage. We see Man at their feet. As they do the Scorpion Squash dance, Man dodges their feet, turning, sliding, escaping, but always at risk. He is behind them one moment, then in the front, among then beyond. It is important that they take risks together. Two separate entities are actually dancing. The folk dancers have become a single body and Man is left as an individual. Once the music is over, he leaves the stage. When he leaves, the team stops, and the heads of two girls from the local group pop out between the linked arms of the male group. It looks as if the men are carrying two women's heads under their arms. The male group and the women perform the steps of the Scorpion Squash dance in that state.

AUDIO. When the team leader signals to start, music begins. The sound of copper being hammered, common in the market district in Diyarbakır, turns into electronic sounds with one echoing on top of the other. These are the only sounds. We do not hear the sound of the dancer's steps. When the girls take their heads out from under the arms of the men, they recite a verse about the men of Diyarbakır. The men recite it with them.

The team leader tells them to disperse, and as they leave, we see that Man and Woman are already at the back of the stage, in position.

SCENE 5

IMAGE. As the team leaves the stage, an image falls on Woman and Man. The still image of a wall, covered in partially torn 1980s-era wallpaper with a pattern of pink flowers. (Same as the video from the Stage I, Scene 1, but without Young Girl.)

PERFORMANCE. Man and Woman stand as they has in Stage I, Scene 2 (in the yard of the church) where the performance began. This is a reference to the beginning of the play. Or this is another view of the same relationship with different details. Woman and Man perform choreographed movements similar to those in the first scene. It is structured like a continuation of, or a deeper look into, the duo's relationship. It involves dangerous movements. Again, the theme of risk-taking is explored. The choreography involves the neck: grabbing the neck, the throat, and dragging.

At one particular moment, Man and Woman both turn their backs to the spectators and face the wall. Woman mumbles the same text in a somewhat scolding manner.

WOMAN. Building a good family makes a person happy. Living without love is like living in a desert. Knowing the joy of sharing is the foundation of the path to peace. Finding one's home, country, is finding peace. Happy kids grow up in happy homes. Beautiful things are nourished by people's hearts. The happy person is the one who shares. The secret of living together happily is being able to hug the other person at even the most difficult moment. The cure for the most critical patient is a hand, reaching out with compassion. The brain of happiness is love, heart its sacrifice, food its sharing . . . (*As Woman tries to climb the wall again*) Leave me . . . Leave me . . . I don't want it. Nobody is listening to me. Leave me be, leave me be. Get out! I don't want to listen to those around me. Nobody's listening to me. No one, no one . . . I don't want to talk. I don't want to deal with anyone. Leave me alone. I am tired, tired, enough, I am tired. I am so tired. I am tired, I am tired. I am so tired. I don't want to see anything. I don't want to help. Ahhh . . . there is a rock on my stomach, take off the rock . . . There is a rock on my stomach, take off the rock. There is a rock on my stomach, take off the rock. I am so tired. I don't want to listen. I don't want to hear. I don't want to help.

Woman is delirious. Man attempts to comfort her.

AUDIO. As Man calms Woman down, street sounds are heard. The inside and outside spaces mingle. Sounds of children from the streets of Diyarbakır, boys playing soccer and yelling. The outside noises inside the space are like the shared memory of Man and Woman.

PERFORMANCE. Woman calms down. Man loses himself in the small movements he has performed to calm Woman down. He forgets about Woman and dances off in his own world. Woman gets up, leans against the wall. She watches Man and yells at him.

WOMAN. I will never tell you that tale.

The lights go out, as does the projected image.

SCENE 6

Man has left the stage. Woman is still on the stage, leaning against the wall. Verbal text and video begin at the same time. In the video, Young Girl (in the headscarf costume) dances with the wall, or sways with the power she draws from the wall. This is projected on Woman onstage. Twice as big, Young Girl dances over and around her.

VIDEO. Long shot of Young Girl (in the headscarf costume). She performs a series of practiced movements around the wall, whcih includes hitting the wall repeatedly with her palms. (*Duration: 1 minute, 5 seconds*)

THIRD-GENERATION WOMAN. —Yes, yes, a lot . . . it's really a bird and this is amazing . . . yes, two birds, mouth to mouth . . . what is this!? (*She is reading someone's fortune at the bottom of their coffee cup.*)

SECOND-GENERATION WOMAN. And asking, asking funny things . . . Like asking, what is two times two . . . I say five . . . says OK . . . you know, like that . . . (*She is talking about her flirting.*)

THIRD-GENERATION WOMAN. It's a wonderful thing to be a woman, especially doing it all together like this . . .

THIRD-GENERATION MAN. I say, "Hey, Mom, you have made love." "Hey," she says, "drop it, close this topic," and so on.

THIRD-GENERATION WOMAN. I'm happy at the moment . . . I guess.

SECOND-GENERATION MAN. My father's father owned four homes.

SECOND-GENERATION WOMAN. I wanted to be different. I wanted to be different in life.

THIRD-GENERATION WOMAN. Loving a lot. I guess that's the most important thing. The solution to everything, I guess.

IMAGE 5.6 **Woman lies on a carpet surrounded by ground meat. Audio recordings of debates on Turkey's admission to the European Union play in the background.**
Esra Bezen Bilgin as Woman.
Home Sweet Home. 14th International Istanbul Theatre Festival, Narmanlı Building in Istanbul, June 2004.
Photograph by Aylin Özmete (Courtesy: IKSV).

Woman on stage moves away from the wall, and starts impro-vised dialogue with the audio text.

FIRST-GENERATION WOMAN. Then here comes Diyarbakır, three years in Diyarbakır . . .

FIRST-GENERATION MAN. Our milk is the milk of Mardin . . .

SECOND-GENERATION MAN. I am going to Istanbul! I am going to Istanbul to live there . . .

FIRST-GENERATION MAN. Our Patrick . . .

FIRST-GENERATION WOMAN. They make us pretty in school, they hand us flowers, bouquets, they say King Michael is coming, the grandson of King Karol . . .

SECOND-GENERATION WOMAN. I am the assistant at the time, so I try to look nice, with my clothes . . . but because I don't have much money ... there is this magazine called *Burda* ... I would cut out patterns from that and sew clothes.

SECOND-GENERATION MAN. There is no food. I got the bread, I put the plain bread in my pocket. I ate it, pinch by pinch.

THIRD-GENERATION MAN. Peace of mind, for instance, is very important ...

A performer from the group of local men enters the stage and starts performing the "Jagged Dance."

THIRD-GENERATION WOMAN. There are no nightmares, no questions ... I mean, there is nothing.

THIRD-GENERATION MAN. Because we have to go through all that difficulty somehow, you know. Like a rat in a maze, one way or another, you find the cheese ...

Another performer from the group of local men enters stage and starts performing the Jagged Dance.

THIRD-GENERATION WOMAN. 1986, '87, '88—those times until '90 were completely apolitical, completely ...

THIRD-GENERATION MAN. And what always happens to me is that ... anyways ... let's skip that stuff ...

A third performer from the group of local men enters stage and starts performing the Jagged Dance.

FIRST-GENERATION WOMAN. We had many nice stories, "happened like this," "so sweetheart, it happens" ...

SCENE 7

As Woman responds to the verbal text, three performers from the group of local men have entered the stage. Four of them do the "Notch Dance" onstage. Each man sings a verse to Woman while the others listen. Once they sing a verse, they notch the floor of the stage with switchblades. And the dance continues.

VERSE 1. I took the fifth step for my future
Curse the power and might that comes with the sixth step
Is it money, the amount and regard of people
Curse the ink of the pen that writes like this

Friend, who is it that they call high society, who are we
What they call high society is science and knowledge
In our life the rich are the sultans
Our bodies are axed, like a carcass
Get away from me friend, if you wish go and become a faggot

VERSE 2. Plum tree in the courtyard, seven sisters are sitting
One of them is the drug of my heart
I can't tell her that
The pergola is painted blue,
Wearing red, lace on her head,
Her tiny nose is nifty,
I can't tell her "I love you."
The thing right by her head,
Not the one at the top but the middle one,
My sun is like my moon,
I cannot say I am embarrassed
Her face is like the full moon,
Her tongue is like sweet honey,
She is like a raft on the Tigris,
I cannot say, "Don't waste time, girl."

VERSE 3. Black hair is braided
She is short and her face is round
It is clear she is not greedy
I swear, brother, I am jealous
Of their white cotton hands
Their slim, gentle waists
The middle of their necks
I swear, brother, I am jealous
Girl, don't you look in the mirror
Don't put clips in your hair
Don't light my heart on fire
I am jealous I am jealous
I am jealous of you, of yourself
Let me go, let me scream
I am jealous of you, of myself

Each one leaves after reciting a verse and scoring the floor until only Woman remains. Woman notches the floor, continues the dance, notches the floor again. Young Girl (in the elementary school uniform) goes onstage. She watches Woman. Woman wants to say something. She notches the floor one more time.

Blackout.

SCENE 8

Man is on the floor, wrapped in a white cloth, like a dead body. In front of him stands Young Girl (in the elementary school uniform). During the text, the Young Girl enters and sits near the "corpse." She watches the corpse for a long time, then touches it, puts her head on its chest, starts lifting and posing it; then she starts acting more freely, gets on top of the corpse, starts playing, as if making out with it. She is, in a way, making love to the dead body. Because the body is limp, she has control over it. She uses it as she wishes. Her body language conveys eroticism.

THIRD-GENERATION WOMAN. I'm telling you, I'm in the car. You're not. I see you. My father is old, so he doesn't see well. My brother is nearsighted, he does not see either. But I do. My vision is crystal clear. Somehow, I can see for my brother . . .

. . . Says, "Ahhh . . . we did not see. Ahhh, how did you not miss it, look I see it . . . "

"I'm also far away . . ."

"You know I'm not that close to the table . . . but I see my brother's name on the list . . . "

"I will somehow have it written somewhere. I will make my voice heard . . . I can't stay still any longer. I've gone crazy. I'm having a nervous breakdown . . . "

"I didn't know . . . Death fast, how would I know. I don't know what kind of a thing it is. I didn't experience it, I didn't see it, or you know I didn't hear it . . . I mean I wanted to do something, I couldn't."

" . . . I mean, I went through a lot . . . I didn't stop. I never stopped."

IMAGE 5.7 **Young Girl in the elementary school uniform plays with the corpse of Man, suggesting necrophilia.**
Su Güneş Mıhladız as Young Girl.
Home Sweet Home. 14th International Istanbul Theatre Festival, Narmanlı Building in Istanbul, June 2004.
Photograph by Aylin Özmete (Courtesy: IKSV).

"My brother asks: 'Why did you come?'"

"I say: 'I came for you,'"

"Damn, are you scared of me? What's more, I'm alone, there is no one else. There is no one by my side. I have gone alone. You know, by my brother's side. You know what I'm saying, why are they intimidated by me, what could be wrong with me?"

"I said, 'I'll meet with him' . . . "

"At one point, I became like him. You know, we take the shuttle to visit, my eyes were staring into space, I was absent-minded. I mean, I forgot everything. I mean, I was not myself, you know . . . He says, 'What's happening, don't space out, it's not good to be absent-minded.' Apparently, being absent-minded is not good for anyone . . . "

"I did, I mean I did what I did. I come and go. And then they start telling me, 'Girl, don't you have anyone?' I said, 'I do, why not?' 'I mean, can you do it?' I said, 'I can do it, I can do anything, just show me how. I can overcome any obstacle.' He said, 'Wow, I'm shocked, I mean, alone, you are a woman, you know.' I said, 'I can do it, why can't I?' I said, 'I have people. I have my mom. I have my dad . . . They're old . . . ' "

"But I still haven't stopped, I'm still trying, I never stopped either. It's still going on . . . I said, 'Show me, I'll do it' . . . OK, I'll do that, too."

"You have power. You can do it. Everything is within your power. He said, 'OK, you go take your brother,' he said . . . OK. I took my brother, brought him, but I still have hope. I knew something would happen. Internally, you know, I said that to myself; hopefully, they will not take him again, despite everything, I had a hope. I never lost hope . . . "

". . . I was so happy, you know? I was screaming, I said, 'You did very good, I mean,' I said, 'May God be pleased with you, thanks, thank you . . .'"

". . . I said, 'Come on, get up, they gave us permission for six months, come on, let's go . . .'"

SCENE 9

Young Girl (in the elementary school uniform) leaves as Woman enters. Several local children enter the stage with Woman. They have made paper airplanes using playbills of the performance. They launch them. Earlier, bats flew across the stage; now it's paper airplanes. As the children launch the planes and have fun, Woman unwraps Man, still shrouded. A video is projected on the stage.

VIDEO. Images of many different spaces are juxtaposed. This is a kind of perception of time. We glide from one space to another. *Audio text starts with the video.*

AUDIO. Someone's fortune is being read. It is simple present tense.

"Yes, you are confused, there are many things . . . a lot of ideas coming out of one another . . . there is an idea for meeting . . . they are all connected . . . There is the meeting of two very serious things here . . . You are confused, your heart is conflicted . . . the things you want, the stories have become intertwined and you're trying to sort these out . . . you will get through this . . .

" . . . However, despite this chaos, everything is woven, like lace . . . the things you want are really tied connected, you succeed in what you want, but that chaos is always there . . . It is so chaotic, you are trying to connect so many things that this is difficult for you . . . will you look here?"

SCENE 10

The stage is empty.

VIDEO. A short film tells a Kurdish folktale. It is a love story, the story of a couple who cannot reach one another. A third person, their enemy, stands in the way of their union. An immortal love, couples separated by death. They bury the woman, the man, and the enemy in the same grave, side by side by side. Because the eternity of love has been realized with the existence of the third person. And for eternity they have to be together.

VIDEO. Young Girl (in the wedding dress) and Group Leader; their body language distinctive. Young Girl waltzes in order to flirt but Group Leader does not respond. He leaves the scene, doing the "Eagle Dance"—a metaphor for arranged marriage.

SCENE 11

When the video ends, Group Leader enters the stage. Following him, the rest of the group enters the stage doing the Eagle Dance. Once they are all onstage, they stand shoulder-to-shoulder at the back, forming a wall. Man is among them. Woman also enters the stage. She positions herself next to them. She wants a place among them. She wants to be part of the picture. She can't find any room. She tries to open up a space among them. She jumps on them. They are like a wall: she climbs on them, trying to go over them. They hold her, put her on the floor. They leave.

SCENE 12

Woman is alone on stage.

AUDIO. The audio text talks to Woman again. This time she does not respond at all, just listens calmly and looks at the spectators.

> FIRST-GENERATION MAN. Anything else you want, my beautiful girl? Come on . . .
>
> *Recording of the performer's own voice:*
>
> "I don't know much but I'm not happy . . . What I want to give is indeed from the beginning to the end there . . . I mean, it's not over yet, on the contrary, in a more meaningful sense, it is just beginning . . .
>
> "I am in a Nazi camp, I am in a circus . . .
>
> "I mean, what he killed, killed him . . .
>
> "It's great to be on stage, it's like mocking life . . . Everything is too fast, sometimes I get tired . . .
>
> "It is a strange period. I wonder what I'll say when I begin talking about our time one day . . .
>
> "I mean something like this, I mean, the meeting of two very serious things is happening here, two very serious things are meeting here. This is indescribable, like the meeting of two lovers. It is not something like this . . . this is something else . . ."

VIDEO. During this, there is the projection of Young Girl (in the wedding dress) on the wall. She has taken the leeches off her hands, but her hands are bleeding. She is looking at her hands, smiling.

PERFORMANCE. The *erbane* group again lines up at the front of the stage like a wall. Woman goes over to them. Together, they move to a different door. The spectators follow. Another threshold has been crossed. Passing through another door, they come to another space.

STAGE III. The Backyard

Performers/spectators are at the side wall of the church. The platform here is at ground level. It has no incline.

PERFORMANCE. The *erbane* players come to the front of the last stage. On the stage behind them, in the small space, a light comes on. The *erbane* players move aside. On the platform is Young Girl (in the wedding dress). She is holding an aquarium. Inside the aquarium swim dozens of leeches. When the spectators are settled, she puts the aquarium down and leaves the stage. Under the lights, the underwater "performances" of the leeches are watched through the aquarium.

The End

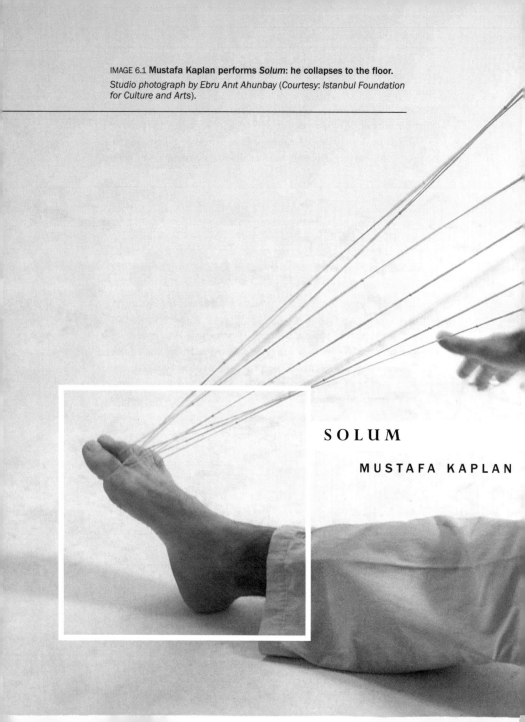

IMAGE 6.1 **Mustafa Kaplan performs *Solum*: he collapses to the floor.**
Studio photograph by Ebru Anıt Ahunbay (Courtesy: Istanbul Foundation for Culture and Arts).

SOLUM

MUSTAFA KAPLAN

NOTE ON THE PLAY

Solum premiered at the 15th Istanbul Culture and Arts Festival, Garaj Istanbul, Istanbul, Turkey, in May 2006.

It is a one-man performance, directed, choreographed, and performed by Mustafa Kaplan.

SOLUM
Mustafa Kaplan

MY BODY IS MY COUNTRY

There is very little light on stage. The spectators can barely see the silhouette of someone walking. The silhouette comes downstage left and waits. For a while, it stands, waiting. It does not attempt any action that may be expected of it.

Images that form the accompanying storyboard are captured by Mark Ventura from a video shot by Nadi Güler. *Solum*, 15th Istanbul Culture and Arts Festival, Garaj Istanbul, Istanbul, May 2006.

The stage is illuminated by light falling centerstage. A man dressed in black becomes visible. He is holding a black case that looks like a make-up bag under his arm. After waiting a little longer, he carefully places the case in the middle of the stage, about three feet away from a stool.

He opens the case, places a handful of rubber bands on either side of the stool. As he places the rubber bands, he sits on the stool on left corner of the stage, facing the audience.

He looks at the rubber bands on the floor. He sees piles, stray rubber

IMAGE 6.2 **Kaplan looks at the rubber bands on the floor.**

IMAGE 6.3 **Kaplan puts on a rubber band as if it were a headband.**

IMAGE 6.4 **Kaplan puts a rubber band across his face.**

IMAGE 6.5 **Kaplan's fingers explore his new face.**

bands. He picks up the one farthest from him. He stretches it a little with his hands and puts it on as if it is a headband.

One side of a second rubber band goes under his chin, the other side over the top of his head. These two rubber bands frame the face. This frame passes below the hairline on the forehead and near the two earlobes and ends under the chin.

The third rubber band goes over the left ear, passes over the nose and is placed so that it will be on the bottom right part of the chin.

The rubber band cuts across the face diagonally: from a distance, the face appears sliced. The fourth rubber band crosses the mouth and is put over the top of the head. This band adds a weird smile to the man whose face is covered in cuts. He places the fifth, sixth, seventh, eighth bands so that they divide the face into many small sections. As he puts on a rubber band as if

(*Facing page*) IMAGE 6.6 **Kaplan begins to divide his face into many small sections with rubber bands.**

Studio photograph by Ebru Anıt Ahunbay (Courtesy: Istanbul Foundation for Culture and Arts).

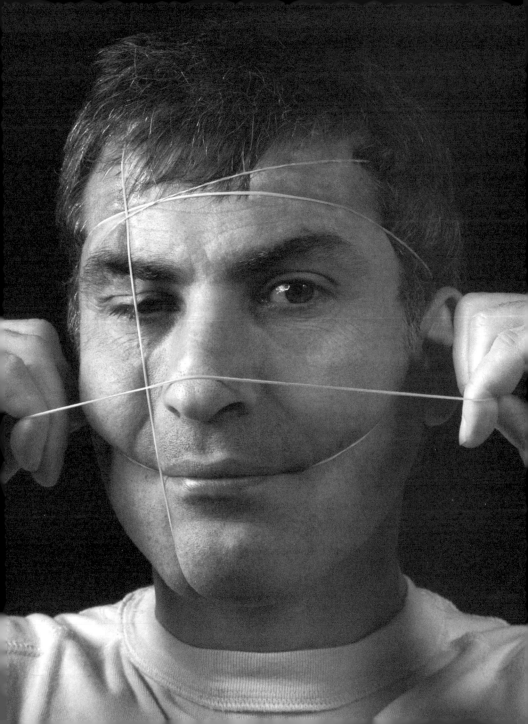

it's a crown, the hands, the fingers look as if they are trying to explore this new face.

This crushed, elongated, stretched, sagging, round thing, full of lines, which give the impression that it is five different faces, is almost ready to speak. He says as much as the bands allow, moving the muscles in his face as much as he can:

My mom used to say that boys don't smile while having their pictures taken . . .
When it was once upon a time, my mom used to talk about genies, elves, and fairies.

"Five-faces-in-one" looks at the left side of his body. He turns the stool on its axis and turns his body to the side so that the spectators can see this thing onstage from the right side too. The dents and bulges formed by the rubber bands are reminiscent of the Aegean coast; the distortion is great.

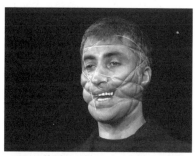

IMAGE 6.8 **Kaplan talks as much as the bands allow.**

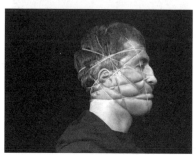

IMAGE 6.9 **Kaplan shows the right side of his face.**

(*Facing page*) IMAGE 6.7 **Kaplan divides his face into many small sections with rubber bands.**

Studio photograph by Ebru Anıt Ahunbay (*Courtesy: Istanbul Foundation for Culture and Arts*).

Five-faces-in-one now puts bands on at random. He puts them on because he *has* to put them on. This is a routine. As he puts the bands on he tries to continue the first sentences he spoke . . .

We did not talk much but we knew what we wanted to say . . . boys should be boys like boys.

At the end of this sentence a bunch of rubber bands are tucked into the mouth.

The bands are then taken out of the mouth one by one and put on anywhere on the head as quickly as possible.

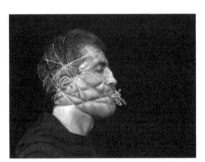

IMAGE 6.10 **Kaplan tucks rubber bands into his mouth.**

As he does this, he completes one rotation on the stool. At the end of the rotation, there is nothing recognizable as a face.

Words spill incoherently from this mouth, if it can still be called a mouth.

Bearded garden, black trees, Mad Yusuf and then . . .

IMAGE 6.11 **Kaplan's face, divided by bands, is not recognizable anymore.**

He turns, so that he now faces the audience again.

    . . . time flew . . .

A rubber band is extended from the left side of the forehead away from the body.

IMAGE 6.12 **Kaplan weaves a series of rubber bands into one long unit.**

IMAGE 6.13 **Kaplan extends the woven rubber bands away from his body.**

    . . . the bearded garden got smaller, the black trees have shrunk, Mad Yusuf has gotten even madder

He takes some bands from his left wrist. He braids them on the left side of the head—if this thing can still be called a head—like a spider weaving its web. The braided bands get longer and longer.

    Mom closed the eyes

This thing, directly facing the spectators now, even though the spectators can no longer bear to watch, looks like a pile of ground meat.

"Looks-like-a-head" pulls a rubber band from the right side of his jaw and extends it to a little under his left breast. He looks at the right side of his body.

> *ready or not, here I come, the*
> *sky and the magma . . .*
> *I could neither go, nor stay*

He says this sentence as he flexes and releases his right bicep; the rubber band extends and contracts.

Then he ties a second rubber band to the left side of his head, which creates tension opposing the first rubber band. He pulls both bands in opposite directions. These bands that are about to break lower the tension of looks-like-a-head.

IMAGE 6.14 **Kaplan pulls bands in opposite directions on his head.**

As blood keeps flowing into the flesh, the "red-flesh/flesh-head" now looks blood red. It has increased the tension created by the hands.

The hands come forward and extends the bands. As the hands are placed on the knees, the flesh-head joins them and falls forward.

The hands are lifted. As the hands go up, the flesh-head joins them and rises. With the stool in the center, the whole body makes a rightward 90-degree turn. And finally the body gets up.

It looks to the right, only because it has to. The bands veil the eyes; even if it looks, it's not possible for it to see clearly. As much as it can tell through the gap between the bands and the light that enters his eye, it estimates the direction and slowly walks to the other station.

IMAGE 6.15 **Kaplan walks to the center of the stage.**

He arrives at the wall. He is no longer within the area of visibility; that thing that is embarrassed to show itself has again become a silhouette. He is comfortable in the dark, hidden in a corner. Again, he waits.

He ties a band on his right hand, also attached to the flesh-head, to another, longer band that's connected to the wall and the "torso" walks to the center of the stage.

IMAGE 6.16 **Kaplan lifts his leg.**

IMAGE 6.17 **Kaplan sinks into a half-squat when the bands can't extend more.**

His gait is reminiscent of a tired old man's. As he walks, the band attached to the flesh-head gets tighter. It extends, extends, and extends. It is about to snap. The torso continues to walk a little farther. He lifts his left leg and crosses it over the right leg at the knee. He sinks into a half-squat in the cross-legged position.

IMAGE 6.18 **Kaplan sinks into a split. His feet are as far apart as possible and the tension between the legs adds to the tension created by the band. His right hand extends the band that is attached to the flesh-head.**

The left leg is then swung around, and put behind him; he sinks into a split. The two feet are as far apart as possible and the tension between the legs adds to the tension created by the band. The right hand extends the band that is attached to the flesh-head.

IMAGE 6.19 **Kaplan sits with his foot tucked underneath, trying to balance the tension on his head and neck.**

The left knee touches the floor. The body is now sitting, with the left foot tucked underneath. The right foot is retracted. The left hand comes to the center.

The right hand, keeping tension on the band, touches a spot on the floor, as far away as it can reach. Rubbing the floor it generates sound.

With sudden decisiveness the whole body thrusts forward. Stopping in a position parallel to the ground. the right hand pulls, rocking the entire body to and fro.

He decides to stop rocking and moves backwards on all fours, going toward the stool. He puts a few more bands on his face and then sits down on the stool.

He pulls the band that connects the wall and the flesh-head and ties it to the stool and after putting a few more bands on his face, ties the free ends of the all the bands attached to his face to the toes of his right foot.

IMAGE 6.20 **With his right hand, keeping tension on the band, Kaplan touches a spot on the floor, as far away as he can reach. He rubs the floor, generating sound.**

IMAGE 6.21 **Parallel to the ground, on his right hand, Kaplan rocks his entire body to and fro.**

IMAGE 6.22 **Kaplan attaches the free ends of the all the bands attached to his face to the toes of his right foot.**

IMAGE 6.23 **Kaplan sits on the stool.**

When he straightens his back, the group of bands that connects the right foot to the face becomes very tense. When he brings his right foot closer to the stool and starts playing with the tense bands with his hands, forms the torso into both a musician and a musical instrument—"double-bass."

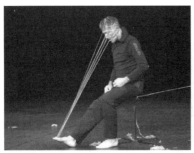

IMAGE 6.24 **Kaplan tests the tension on the bands that connect his foot to his face.**

IMAGE 6.25 **Kaplan plays the tense bands with his hands. His body becomes both a musician and a musical instrument, "double-bass."**

IMAGE 6.26 **Kaplan plays the tense bands with his hands.**

(*Facing page*) IMAGE 6.27 **Rubber bands stretch from Kaplan's face to his foot.**

Studio photograph by Ebru Anıt Ahunbay (Courtesy: Istanbul Foundation for Culture and Arts).

He tries to whistle by puckering his lips; instead of a whistle it sounds like "tssssıussss . . . tıssssıuuıııhhh . . . ttıııuuufffiıııuu." He cannot manage to whistle.

He starts singing; a little distorted, disjointed, but sings nevertheless:

> *It is evening, I am gloomy again*
> *I am in yearning for the color of your eyes*

The hands keep playing the double-bass/head-bass.

> *Come my full moon come my lover come again*
> *I am in yearning for the color of your eyes*

IMAGE 6.28 **Kaplan sings with his distorted mouth.**

This is remembrance of the wind that licks and caresses our necks, the smell of the sea, the trips. This is mocking the terrifying look of the image, this is the double-bass mocking itself.

IMAGE 6.29 **Kaplan as the double-bass stands on its left foot at the end of the song. Because his right foot is connected to his head, it cannot touch the floor without pulling his head down.**

The double-bass stands on its left foot at the end of the song. Because his right foot is connected to his head, it cannot touch the floor.

Jumping on his left foot, he comes centerstage, pulls another band, which has been hanging from the ceiling. Then he makes his way to the right front corner of the stage and attaches it to the floor.

The stage space has been divided, cut, torn with the second band. These two bands, as much as tearing the stage, have formed their own fields of force around them with the tension they bear.

After this connection, the double-bass covers his head with the hood of his black clothes. Only the contours can be seen now. His head, and the destruction the bands have caused, are now hidden.

IMAGE 6.30 **Kaplan as the double-bass covers his head with his hood hiding his face.**

A bundle of extended bands coming from under black cloth, and the foot attached to it, create a new being. The "furniture-body," which now looks like a statue or a piece of furniture, walks backwards slowly and rhythmically. He stops a bit later, extends his right hand forward, and retracts it suddenly as if it has touched something hot. He starts jumping and shaking his whole body.

IMAGE 6.31 **Kaplan jumps.**

He falls on the floor. There on his back, he rocks back and forth for a while. Because the bands that are attached to the right foot pull the head to the foot, the body takes an elliptical form. With the rhythm of the movement—furniture-body has taken the form of a rocking chair.

IMAGE 6.32 **Kaplan's body takes the form of a rocking chair.**

IMAGE 6.33 **Kaplan springs into a semi-split.**

IMAGE 6.34 **Kaplan transfers some rubber bands to his left foot balancing their tension and rolls to his side.**

When the rocking chair stops, the toes of the left foot skillfully remove a few of the bands that are attached to the toes of the right foot, without help from the hands. Now, both feet have bands on them. When "shape/double" straightens out and rolls onto his side, he looks like a character in a science-fiction movie. The only thing missing is a light saber in its hand.

The shape/double stands up, his back to the spectators. Slowly, as he turns to face the spectators, he expands one of the bands with his left hand. First, his right hand passes through the opening created by the extended band. Then his entire body follows the hand. Shape/double is trying to pass through the double-bass; the outside and the inside are intertwined.

IMAGE 6.35–36 **Kaplan's hands try to pass through his new body.**

At the end of this process, the bands have become a coil of inside/outside, up/down, and double bass. He goes to the black box.

He takes a pair of scissors out of the black box, then sits on the box.

The hood is slowly taken off. The spectators see that thing again: five-faces-in-one, looks-like-a-head, flesh-head, double-bass. The flesh that has been cut into sections by the lines made by the bands trembles in different rhythms as pieces separate from one another. He cannot control the shaking of the flesh.

He takes the tip of the scissors in his right hand to his forehead, and in order to cut a bit of the band that has settled rather deeply into the flesh by now, he searches in the space between the skin and the flesh; if he finds one, he immediately cuts it; if he cannot, he continues searching. He searches sometimes in his hair, under his chin, around his eyes, and sometimes inside his mouth.

 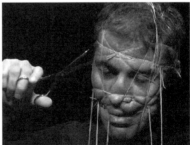

IMAGE 6.37–38 **Kaplan cuts the bands wrapped around his head.**

Once the bands have been cut, disintegrated, dispersed, taken off and have sprung to different parts of the space, the "face/head" relives the whole process backwards. The muscles and the skin get crushed, puckered, drained, relaxed one more time. During this process, the thousand and one faces are repeated in reverse. Once the last band has been cut, only the marks remain.

IMAGE 6.39 **The rubber bands are gone but their marks remain on Kaplan's face.**

He works his way through the bands in between his toes. Leaning forward, he shakes off the severed bands and hair, causing them to fall onto the ground. He cleans up.

Again, he picks up two rubber bands from the floor and stands up straight. He comes to the right-front corner of the stage and waits. For a while, without attempting any action that may be expected of him, he stands, waiting.

The marks on his face from the dozens of bands are deep. As the marks start reverting back to normal, the skin moves. Blood flows a little faster in these marks to make up for the difference. The skin wants its color back. It knows where the marks come from. It wants this information to live as long as possible. This is a battle between the marks and the body, even if there is some back-and-forth movement in this process, it is always in the direction of the disappearance of the marks. This moment of waiting shows respect to the marks.

IMAGE 6.40 **Kaplan sings the second song.**

The two rubber bands in his hand are quickly passed over the head and left on the neck. The bands squeeze the neck. And then the second voice/song comes:

> *On the way to Adana,*
> *the cotton are on their*
> *branches*
> *may God take my life*
> *in the arms of that lover*

This song is also a mark, a reminder from his childhood. The shiny, shimmering pebbles he swallowed as a kid and his friend who tried to circumcise himself with nippers, disappear in the joyful rhythm of this folk song.

With a sudden movement, he lays down on his back on the stage. He goes on singing the folk song.

Hey girl from Adana
I am burnt, you flirtatious
    thing
in the Adana market
one cannot go around
    alone

As he is on the floor on his back, singing the folk songs, he puts both his hands in front of his chest and with his fingertips, he starts playing his ribcage like a drum. He sings as he does this.

Are you a bush right there
are you the branch of the
    bush
when there are youth
    available
would you take the old one

IMAGE 6.41 **Kaplan plays his ribcage like a drum while singing.**

During this, between him beating himself and beating the drum, the sound that comes from the body that is singing the song, and getting beaten, joins with another rhythm that he cannot control—as he does this "song-voice" gets distorted, disjointed, warped.

One more time the body becomes both the one that is played and the one that sings.

As he continues to lay on the floor on his back, singing and playing himself, the right arm moves from the side of his head opposite the direction of his feet. Suddenly, he flips onto his stomach and stops singing.

He raises his right arm as though he's holding a weapon and raises the upper body off the floor a little following the right arm.

IMAGE 6.42 **Kaplan places his arms as if he is holding a weapon.**

The stomach and the pelvis are on the floor, the right knee is bent, the right foot is over the left foot. The left leg is stretched longer and both legs are a little further over the floor. In this state, he looks like a toy soldier in a prone position. He looks left and right and his body sways too.

This moving body starts rocking on its stomach back and forth. This motion is reminiscent of a rocking chair. What he had done with furniture-body earlier, he does with curve-body on his stomach.

IMAGE 6.43 **Kaplan is like a toy soldier in a prone position.**

With this rhythmic movement, he turns 180 degrees, and stays like that for a moment. Curve-body looks left and right. And, releasing all the tension in his muscles, sticks to the floor, gets lost in it, stays there for a moment.

Curve-body gets up slowly. In the process he takes off the hooded T-shirt he is wearing. After he has taken off the T-shirt, the cuts that have been formed with the bands from the joint of the arms and the shoulder, his neck and his waist become visible.

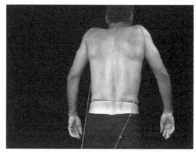

IMAGE 6.44 **The lines of the rubber bands separate the torso, head and the arms from one another, making it look like a plastic body.**

These lines/cuts make the head, the torso, and the arms appear separate from one another. This is a plastic body; this is a body where the arms and the head can be taken off and put back on at any moment.

This "plasti-body," carefully places the T-shirt on the rear right corner, about a yard away from the stool. He picks up two separate bands from the floor, puts one over each shoulder. He slowly sits down on the stool, with his back towards the spectators.

As the plasti-body sits on the stool, the only recorded music of the performance is heard, the sound of music coming from a great distance: the clinking of a   wedding bell in a far-away village. Slowly, as the wedding party approaches, the

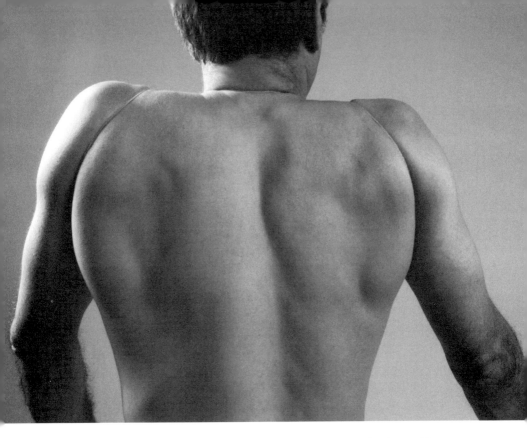

IMAGE 6.45 **Rubber bands divide Kaplan's head, torso and arms.**

Studio photograph by Ebru Anıt Ahunbay (Courtesy: Istanbul Foundation for Culture and Arts).

music becomes louder, and is more comprehensible.

yabanlıdan gel,
karada güldü yarim,
yabandanda,
aslanımda gel, gel,

yaban yürü,
serdim kiri,
cümbüş teli,
gerdim zili,

amaaaaaaannnnn,
aldım haberinide,
garib, garib çobandan,
aslanımda gel, gel,
aman yürü, yürü,
kostak yürü, yürü,
serseri yürü, yürü

As the plasti-body descends toward the stool, the shoulders rise. When the buttocks touch the stool, the shoulders have risen as high as possible. The ribcage goes back, then left, as the knees go right. The ribcage and the knees return to their original positions. The head falls forward, disappears between the shoulders. Then, as the shoulders descend, the head takes its place again. Each piece of the body speaks for itself.

The shoulders join the wedding party with the rhythm of the music and, a while later, they make the plasti-body stand up from the stool. Tied to the chair with bands from each shoulder, the plasti-body takes a few steps and continues to dance.

IMAGE 6.46 **Kaplan, looking like a plastic body, dances.**

This action which seems to be between doing and not-doing, an effort to accompany a rhythmic, lively folk song with a fragmented, mottled body and the stool that it drags along, attached to it by the bands.

Along with this village song, this person who has tied himself to the chair and the stage with bands goes down onto the floor while dancing on his knees. Through rhythmic movements, he puts his head on the floor and lifts his feet off the floor. He stands on his head but the rhythm and dance continue.

His feet finally go down and he lies on the floor face down, legs together, hands to his sides.

IMAGE 6.47 **Kaplan lays on the floor, face down.**

He waits for the music to end. He extends both arms forward and gets good traction on the floor. Pressing down on the floor with his hands, he pulls his whole body forward. He repeats this movement a few times. The stool, attached to him by the bands, follows a few of these forward movements by sliding on the floor.

Finally he reaches the corner. He puts his head on the floor again and does a headstand.

IMAGE 6.48–49 **Kaplan is upside down in the corner, the bands pull the stool towards him.**

He leans his back, hips, and feet on the wall, slowly lifts his hands off the floor.

He is now seeing it all reversed. From his point of view, the entire stage is upside down. From the point of view of the spectators, the bands and the stool are still in their normal position. The only one whose orientation has changed is the "song-self" that is preparing for the last song.

When the song-self is on his head, the hands slowly go up. First they stop by his legs, then meet on his navel, and in this position, he sings his last folk song.

 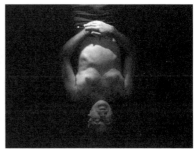

IMAGE 6.50–51 **Kaplan sings his last song while standing solely on his head.**

ferayiiiiiiiii, kuuuzuunnn,
aaaaaaaaduuu,
ferraaaaaaaayyyiiiiiiddeed
  deeddee,
yar, yandımm,
ammaaaaaaaaaaaan,
essmeerr yaarimde, amanda
yandım,
feraaaayyiiiii,

ninnaaa nniinnnaaa
nninnaa, ninnnaaa,
ninnnnaaaaa yaaaarr,
niinnaaaaa, ninnnnaaaa
yaaarrr,
amanda yandım
fereaaaaaaiyyyyiiiii

As the half-naked man sings the folk song, in this topsy-turvy, head-stand, upside-down pose, his hands seek something along his body. They find one of the bands that are attached to the stool. He breaks it, holds it in his hand for a moment, then releases it. The rubber band was taut and, when released, shoots from one end of the stage to the other. This is an instantaneous movement and makes a sound like this:

vviiiiiiiiiiiiiiiiiiinnnnnn

The End

MURATHAN MUNGAN

Murathan Mungan, one of Turkey's most revered contemporary poets, received his BA and MA in Theater from Ankara University. He has published poems, stories, essays, reviews, and novels, and his plays have been staged and praised both in Turkey and abroad. He has also worked as an editor and a dramaturge and directed festivals and shows. Since 1988, he has lived and worked as a freelance writer in Istanbul. Mungan has also written radio plays, three screenplays and directed plays by other playwrights. One of his screenplays, *Dağınık Yatak* (Messy Bed), was filmed in 1984 by Atıf Yılmaz. His work has been translated into and published in 14 languages.

Mungan's first staged play, *Bir Garip Orhan Veli* (The Poet Orhan Veli) was performed for over 20 years. His seminal theatrical work is the *Mesopotamian Trilogy*. The three plays, *Mahmud and Yezida*, *Taziyeh* (Condolences), and *Geyikler Lanetler* (Deer Curses) were performed separately in Turkey and abroad and were published simultaneously in separate volumes.

A collection of his plays, including *As on the Page*, entitled *Kâğıt Taş Kumaş* (Paper Rock Cloth) was published in 2007. *As on the Page* wass part of "1001 Nights," a collective project that brought together writers from across the Middle East at the Betty Nansen Theater in Copenhagen. It was also performed in 2005 at the Nottingham Playhouse in the UK as part of series called "1001 Nights Now," which put together eight texts by writers of Middle Eastern origin around the theme of immigration.

TUNCER CÜCENOĞLU

Tuncer Cücenoğlu, who writes almost exclusively for the theater, has authored over 20 plays. The seniormost and most widely performed playwright represented in this anthology, Cücenoğlu serves on the boards of several institutions and works as a professor of Dramatic Playwriting. He has won many awards, both in Turkey and abroad. He aims for an international audience in his plays, universalizing his plays by addressing global themes.

Almost all his plays have been published and performed in Turkey and have been translated into several languages including Russian, English, German, French, Arabic, and Persian. Several of his plays have been performed in more than 40 countries.

Avalanche has been translated into 15 different languages. It was first performed in Poland, and then in Turkey, Russia, Georgia, Bulgaria, Azerbaijan, Romania, and Kazakhstan. In Russia it has won several awards and was performed in five theaters simultaneously.

ŞAHİKA TEKAND

Şahika Tekand is an award-winning director, teacher, and playwright. Tekand dropped out of law school before enrolling in acting school, and went on to earn a Ph.D. in Theater and Acting from Dokuz Eylül University in İzmir, Turkey. She has also appeared in 18 films. Tekand founded the acting school "Studio" in 1988, which has played an important role in Turkey in actor training as an alternative to traditional conservatory training. She teaches and trains students not only at Studio but also in several private universities' theater departments that have been established in Istanbul over the past decade.

In 1990 Tekand founded her own ensemble, Studio Oyuncuları (The Studio Players). The plays they have staged include five that she wrote and directed herself, all of which were invited to several national and international festivals.

In 2002, Tekand began adapting the tragedies of Sophocles as part of her *Oedipus Trilogy*. With *Oedipus Rex* in mind, she wrote and directed *Where is Oedipus?* (2002); and *Oedipus in Exile* (2004) was based on *Oedipus in Colonos*. In 2006, she wrote her sixth play, an adaptation of Sophocles's *Antigone*, named *Evridike'nin Çığlığı* (*Eurydice*'s *Cry*). This was the third and final play of the trilogy. The play met with huge success in the 15th International Istanbul Theater Festival (2006). She directed the play and performed the role of Eurydice.

ÖZEN YULA

Recipient of several awards, Özen Yula is mainly recognized in Turkey as a playwright even though he has also worked as a director and performer. Yula graduated high school in Oregon, US, and earned an MA in Theater from Ankara University. In 2010, he was a teaching artist in residence in Cleveland, US.

Several of Yula's plays have been translated into English, Italian, German, French, Bulgarian, Finnish, Polish, Japanese, and Russian. They have been performed in France, Sweden, Cyprus, Germany, Austria, England, Holland, Japan, Italy and Egypt. His plays have represented Turkey during the Bonn Biennale and the kontext:Europa festival in Vienna. In Turkey, they have been published in a four-volume anthology.

For Rent has been staged as a reading in Italy, France, and Germany in renowned venues such as Schaubühne am Lehniner Platz. In 2008, Mauro Avogadro directed the play in Asti and Trento, Italy, and, in 2009, it was performed as part of the event "Around the World in 24 Hours" hosted by the Internationalists.

EMRE KOYUNCUOĞLU

Emre Koyuncuoğlu is not only a prolific director, dramaturge, and writer, but also a dancer and choreographer. She has an MA in Dramaturgy and Theater Criticism from Istanbul University. She co-founded the ensemble Yeşil Üzümler (Green Grapes) in 1991 with Mustafa Kaplan. She has worked as a dramaturge for the Izmit City Theater since 1997. Her independent productions, including original works such as *Misfit* and *Home Sweet Home,* have been performed at various venues in Europe. She had brief residencies as a young artist at the Royal Court in London and also at Schaubühne in Berlin, where she worked as a director's assistant for Thomas Ostermeier.

Koyuncuoğlu has written for theater journals and newspapers in Turkey, and has contributed to international publications. She has taught in several colleges and also collaborated with artists from various disciplines in different projects.

MUSTAFA KAPLAN

Mustafa Kaplan is one of the most influential names in contemporary dance and dance theater in Turkey. His work has been praised all over Europe. He trained a generation of dance and dance-theater performers in Istanbul in the past decade.

Kaplan trained in engineering though he has never held a job as an engineer. He started taking dance classes in 1984 and, in 1990, joined the Istanbul Municipal Theater as a choreographer. He researched movement with the actors in the Theater Research Lab, an institution within the Istanbul Metropolitan Municipality City Theater. He is among the founders of several companies that have played significant roles in performance in Turkey, such as Yeşil Üzümler (Green Grapes), Dance Factory, and Çatı (Roof). He has mostly performed his own creations but has also danced in pieces by other choreographers, inlcuding Aydın Teker.

Between 2005 and 2009, *Solum* was performed in many venues and festivals, in Turkey, Germany, Romania, Italy, Brazil, Spain, France, Belgium, Switzerland, and Slovenia.